C. S. Lewis

C. S. Lewis

The Shape of His Faith and Thought

Paul L. Holmer

SHELDON PRESS
LONDON

First published in the United States in 1976
by Harper & Row Inc
10 East 53rd Street, New York, N.Y. 10022

First published in Great Britain in 1977
by Sheldon Press
Marylebone Road, London NW1 4DU

Second impression 1979

Printed in Great Britain by
The Camelot Press Ltd, Southampton

ISBN 0 85969 115 2

TO PHYLLIS

". . . our prospect for life, a prospect which, as it is beheld with more attention, seems to open more extensive happiness, and spreads by degrees into the boundless regions of eternity."

Samuel Johnson, *The Rambler*

FOREWORD

Because we find a completion of our enjoyment in saying why an author is so good, no end of valuations of C. S. Lewis have been written. The valuators have, for the most part, done little to satisfy the desire of thousands of admirers to have Lewis's genius explained. Humbler critics have rarely soared any higher than writing mere paraphrases of what Lewis has already said so much clearer. Other critics, judging Lewis from some partial perspective of their own, have assumed a critical position higher than they have a right to. Because I relish every word that Lewis has written, I have been watching this from the wings, hoping that someday I might succeed where others have failed—hoping I could say exactly what is this giant surplus value in Lewis's writings which makes him perhaps the best theologian of this century and the illuminator of everything he wrote about. Just as I was beginning to believe that the thing would never get done, *C. S. Lewis: The Shape of His Faith and Thought* was put into my hands. It is beyond anything I ever hoped for. Lewis spoke of the 'guiding thread' which runs through all his books—religious, literary, philosophical—and Professor Holmer has shown exactly how all the books are tied together. More importantly, he has produced an assessment of Lewis's works which so completes the pleasure of reading him that I regard Professor Holmer's book as displaying a genius which, in its own way, is not inferior to Lewis's own. This is the best book ever written about Lewis and a valuable and reliable commentary on twentieth-century thought. But here I have come full circle: never having been able to write the one, final, perfect appreciation of C. S. Lewis, I am offended that I haven't the skill to write a satisfactory one about Professor Holmer's book—a work which is absolutely necessary to a full appreciation of C. S. Lewis and one which it would be folly to ignore.

Oxford   WALTER HOOPER

Contents

PUBLISHER'S NOTE

Three of the books by C. S. Lewis referred to in this volume were published in Great Britain by Geoffrey Bles under different titles.

They are:

Case for Christianity published as *Broadcast Talks* (1942).
Weight of Glory published as *Transposition and Other Addresses* (1949).
God in the Dock published as *Undeceptions* (1971).

Other books cited have been published in Great Britain under the same titles.

Preface

THIS BOOK IS WRITTEN partly to discharge a debt incurred during the early days of World War II. An angry and impetuous letter was sent to Mr. C. S. Lewis at Oxford. A lengthy response came; and it was so full of charity and plain wisdom that it made at least this then frustrated and distraught student see very clearly how tangled his own life actually was. That was many years ago; and a lifetime of concern with logical issues, on the one side, and moral and religious-Christian concerns, on the other, have made Lewis's writings, of all kinds, both more interesting and more profound than they initially seemed to me.

In all of his works, fictional, critical, poetical, historical, and apologetical, there is a wisdom to be learned. It is not always in the lines but, rather, between them. I can in no wise ferret it out, for that would betray his authorship and indulge an unfitting pretense. At least I will try to point it out, so that Lewis's reader will discover how much can be learned by reading and rereading them. This has to do with what moderns call the "grammar" of thought on the variety of his topics. That morphology becomes most apparent in theological and Christian matters. But, it is a shaping of reflection that goes on also

in his understanding of what literature is and does, of his grasp
of our common human nature, and certainly in the view he
provides of the moral life. In a peculiar way, the very form of
his literary career begins to limn that wisdom for us. That such
a wisdom is declared overtly in religious writings is no secret
to readers of Lewis.

My debts are many. Several College Seminars in Berkeley
College at Yale University, and lectures at the Yale Divinity
School, Wheaton College, the College of Wooster, and other
places have given occasion for some of these pages. Walter
Hooper, Clyde Kilby, and Tad Stashwick deserve special
thanks. My debts to the scholarly literature about Lewis will be
manifest, I suspect, throughout. The help of Mrs. Nancy Wag-
ner in preparing the manuscript was not unnoticed.

PAUL L. HOLMER

The Divinity School
Yale University

ONE

Some Reminders About Lewis and His Literature

MOST READERS of these pages will probably already know that C. S. Lewis (1898–1963) was, and still is, one of the very popular writers on religious topics. Oddly enough, his works on Christianity, while widely appealing, are rather stringent and severe, mostly because the story of Jesus itself—his birth, life, death, and resurrection—is full of tragedy, sin, misunderstanding, and temptation. Lewis did not find Christianity easy to believe, and his works make quite clear why our tangled lives, like those of the first century, give many reasons for dismissing the whole business as an unnecessary burden.

The Screwtape Letters (1942), still his most popular piece, along with *The Case for Christianity, The Abolition of Man, Miracles,* and *The Problem of Pain,* do something quite different from most books that recommend religion to the modern reader. Instead of insisting that religion will give you what you need in modern twentieth-century terms—no miracles, no taxing commitments, no heaven and hell, and a new policy that will ensure equity, justice, and peace—Lewis delineated the long-standing need we all have for a very tough and virtue-guarded personal life. Along with that and fitting it at every point, he revived the biblical account of a moral and holy God, of Jesus performing miracles and being resurrected from the dead, and a story of salvation on behalf of sinful mankind. All kinds of old things fell into place in his writings, and the entire content and shape of the Christian teaching began to take on a vivacity it did not seem to have in other contexts.

This stream of witty yet fervent literature drew the attention of numerous readers to a Christianity that was not quite liberal, conservative, fundamentalistic, or conventional. The familiar adjectives seemed irrelevant. In fact, it was not as if Christianity were being recommended as either a large-scale social answer or a panacea for personal difficulties. Instead something un-ceremoniously obvious to all of us, namely, our singular inability to make sense of our lives and our longstanding wish for a responsible and resilient kind of happiness, these were plainly and intimately addressed. Both a kind of morals that spoke to such long-standing conditions, plus a tough-minded Christianity, were declared in his pages.

Certainly it was surprising to read a graceful and able writer who could make Aristotle's and Plato's words about ethical matters, especially about virtues and vices, seem like something other than an old and antiquated batch of irrelevant theory. Lewis wrote about them as if they were addressing anyone who was not succeeding in the business of living and who needed a little help. It was flattering, too, to think again that those vener-able teachers, like ourselves, were after the truth on these mat-ters. In any case, without adapting the faith to the dreadful war in which the world was immersed, without suggesting that Aristotle and Plato were alien and ancient Greeks, Lewis pointed to a wisdom that we had all forgotten and to a deeper common plight of which we were only dimly aware.

If it was a surprise to have Aristotelian virtues proved to be always relevant, it was also unusual to have Christian literature and its issues juxtaposed against people in the way Lewis did. Lewis's pages were poetical and pleasurable, yet they also made a stern claim for the truth of Christian teachings. It was not as if Lewis were only a more subtle counselor or as if Christianity were but a psychological gratification. His point, instead, was that all of us were in need of making sense of ourselves, our thoughts, and our behavior, and that both morals and Christianity spoke to that plain condition. Lewis would have it that the Christianity of miracles, of creation, fall, judgment, incarnation, resurrection, heaven and hell, was both true and relevant. It seemed a very new thing to have imagination brought to the aid of strict reasoning and downright wit united with logical vigor. Who then was this C. S. Lewis?

Lewis was from the early years of World War II through the mid-fifties the most widely read Christian apologist writing in English. He never exploited the war, nor did he design a faith for foxholes. In fact, his letters and conversations indicated a detailed awareness of the progress of that war and all that it involved for both sides. Lewis had fought and was injured in the artillery in 1917–18, and his home was a haven for displaced children during the second war. A friend had been killed in action with Lewis and the obligation to care for that friend's mother and sister rested with Lewis until the 1950s. Lewis's apologetic literature for Christian faith, written for the most part while the second war raged but seldom alluding to it, was not written in blissful oblivion of the social malaise of the time. The complaint that concentration camps, the blitz, historical crises, and social devastation do not come into focus in Lewis's literature has been often made. So too the charge that Lewis was offering an escapist faith and a more antiquated attempt at an irrelevant certitude.[1]

I shall be arguing something else. While it seems to me that Lewis's wide appeal could indeed be nothing more to some

1. Alistair Cooke, "Mr. Anthony at Oxford" (a review of *Christian Behavior* and *Perelandra*), *New Republic,* CX (1944): 578–80. Graham Hough, *"The Screwtape Letters:* How Well Have They Worn?" *London Times,* (February 10, 1966), p. 15.

readers than a convenient nostrum that offers simplicities and certainties where none are to be had, that surely says more about the readership than about Lewis's work. His books contain no slick answers and no formulae; there is nothing grandiose promised about conversion or about believing in the Bible that would give solace to the careless or indulgence to the unreliable. More than that, there is nothing in his pages that links Christianity to an optimistic hope for nations, for social movements, or for the utopian wishes of mankind. That kind of celestial warrant for a life of civility, culture, and moral-political synthesis is simply not there. On the other hand, there is little of that misuse of Scripture to remove doubt or that silly notion that we can have peace, contentment, and certainty by becoming a tiny enclave of "true" but anti-intellectual believers immune from the world and its problems. Both the extremes of a biblical socialized Christianity, on the one hand, and of a radically conservative theology are completely eschewed. The will to believe under such auspices and motivation is cut off very quickly in Lewis's pages.

But that "something else" to which I alluded earlier is harder to state. It is related, I think, to Lewis's appeal to Samuel Johnson's words in *The Rambler:*

> We are all prompted by the same motives, all deceived by the same fallacies, all animated by hope, obstructed by danger, entangled by desire, and seduced by pleasure. . . . The main of life is, indeed, composed of small incidents and petty occurrences: of wishes for objects not remote and grief for disappointments of no fatal consequence, of insect vexations . . . , impertinences . . . , of meteorous pleasures. . . . Such is the general heap out of which every man is to cull his own condition. . . .[2]

For Lewis himself this meant a long and arduous endeavor to understand. His literature disguises in its almost effortless

---

2. These sentences are from essays numbered 60 and 68 in *The Rambler* (Everyman edition, 1967), pp. 133, 140–141.

prose the detailed knowledge that it commands. A rare wisdom about people gives Lewis firsthand access both to morals and to Christian literature and thought. In turn, his writings have a way of fitting every reader too. I believe it is this comprehensive understanding that works so well for Lewis; and I shall be at pains in subsequent chapters to show how it manifests itself. But herewith, we can return again to consideration of more features of that apologetic literature itself.

II

Lewis's apologetic literature is posited on a very detailed knowledge of human nature. He is not concerned with it in the gross, either as described by general theories or as subsumed under grand social groupings. That is why the battles between the Allies and the Axis were not as poignant and as revealing to him as the ever present conflicts between the passions and the struggles between vices and virtues. Seeing Christianity in relation to spectacular wickedness is a requirement, of course; but the firsthand materials, the resentments, pique, envy, despair that course through our lives give us our major jolts, engender our wretchedness, and magnify our pettiness into social disaster. By mingling much with the shades of character and developing a discriminating eye for human proclivities, Lewis can rather easily observe how vices and virtues take root in us and why the Devil and God can make the ordinary human heart their field.

This is, of course, to note that Lewis's apologetic literature is in conflict with the main streams of theology and popular religion in the twentieth century. Clearly, Lewis was at home with the New Testament, the church fathers, and a kind of orthodoxy and ordering of the intelligence and affections that comes with a historical liturgy, the creeds, and the humbling worship of God Almighty. The strange side of this to many readers is the air of discovery that Lewis brought to all these matters. Here he is, an exciting and learned wit, full of crackling knowledge about myths, "naturalism," and modernity, who feels not the slightest need to invoke any of these to reformulate or to realign faith and morals. One finds little about symbolism, ontology, and modern man in his literature. At first it looks as though he may not know about all this current thought and is simply being obtusely old-fashioned. But more reading shows a depth to his polemics that is more than entertaining. Lewis succeeds in making Christianity something more than a hobby. It becomes momentous, if for no other reason than the fact that one cannot believe it unless one straightens out all kinds of other thoughts too. It has requisites and makes demands; one has to think it through clearly, and with a critical eye toward the dozens of competing philosophies and myriad outlooks projected for the current reader.

Despite appearances, Lewis was certainly not naïve on theological matters. Because he was not impressed with modern biblical criticism and because, too, he almost never mentioned the big names in modern religion (Temple, Niebuhr, Bultmann, Barth, Kierkegaard) or the major "isms" (existentialism, process-thought, fundamentalism, positivism, let alone idealism, analysis, etc.), it looks as if he were deciding important matters in terms altogether different from those employed by most pedagogues in university and religious circles. The point is, manifestly, that he was. He believed, altogether rightly, that the pedagogical and scholarly conclusions and methods had a very limited role indeed, and that the decisions as to "what" to believe and "whether" to believe were logically independent of these points of views, hypotheses, options, and philosophies by which contemporary readers were both dazzled and rendered hapless to decide. The issues were undecidable in the terms thus proposed. Therefore, it is the aim of Lewis to say whatever he has to say in ways that will not make it one more option and another unheard-of possibility.

My point in stressing this is to make it clear that C. S. Lewis is not espousing fundamentalism under a new literary guise, nor modernism under orthodox rubrics, nor Anglicanism as if it were sectarian, nor morals as if they were Aristotelian, nor existentialism as if it were catholic all along. He does, instead, make a case for the forgotten strategy of achieving the capacities and abilities that rightly belong to our common human nature. Unlike the existentialists, and some Christian writers whom he superficially resembles, Lewis does not believe that the human subject is chiefly and fundamentally a sliver of "will." In the face of the insuperable difficulty of having to decide where the issues are objectively undecidable, one kind of contemporary reflection has taken a desperate way, namely, of proposing that where the options are all even, there we must valiantly, and arbitrarily, choose. Then the human subject looks as if it were doomed to inability and forced into inactivity by the genuine alternatives and equally attractive options.

When morals and Christianity are put into such contexts as they have been in the twentieth century, then they, too, look "relative," without objective warrant, and pertinent only if one dares to choose them. Everything decisive seems to depend upon the will and the decision itself, and the human subject dangles outside these options until he or she can effect the transition by sheer willpower. Plainly, what is here sketched is not so much another theory as it is a predicament we all suffer. Lewis suffered it, too, and chose not to counter it with one more theory but to address it in an indirect manner. Finally, he would have us remember that being a human is not to be already a subject; it is to be so constituted that we make ourselves into subjects. We become increasingly capable, perceptive, sensitive, knowledgeable, able, empowered, and emotionally qualified. Aristotle noted that youthfulness might disqualify some from making moral judgments; and Scripture reminds all readers that the pure in heart will see God and says little on behalf of those who are not thus modified. Capabilities, powers, and abilities have to be achieved before we can see, know, think, love, cherish, grieve over, and enjoy.

Once all of that is remembered, the task of the author with an evangelical intent is altogether different. It is not as if one can rest assured with the age that Christianity is outmoded or that chronology alone has made all old teachings arcane. There are no comforting assurances that time is on one side rather than another or that development and progress have lifted us to new moral heights. Neither are we left with the other kind of irrationality of having to decide blindly because there is nothing rational to give us credentials. Instead, that writer must now address the subject in a way that will increase his or her capacities and strengthen self-cognizance. Only by knowing oneself and effecting one's abilities, bringing them to birth, can one so qualify the self and the subject that truly objective judgments and true seeing of what is what will become feasible.

And that is precisely what Lewis does. That is why his apologetic literature is finally so different. Even though he writes a little book called *The Case for Christianity,* still the thrust is not just in the argument. There is, indeed, an argument and a strong plea for rationality; but it is also the case that one must realize a sense of dismay and see Christian things in that qualified way so that the teachings begin to make sense. Also one must correct self-conceit and self-will by becoming a repentant subject before one can see some things to be the case.[3] It is as if the argument does not begin to gather its force until the reader has realized something about himself. Therefore, the whole picture of rationality itself and what is involved in being responsibly objective becomes deeply hedged.

More particularly, though, one begins to see all over again why morality and religion are so intimately linked. Lewis begins one of his books by showing that simply remembering what we need, namely, being able to get along without conflicts of wish, purpose, and goals and being able to get along with oth-

3. *The Case for Christianity.* (New York: Macmillan, 1943), pp. 27, 49.

ers, that these simple acts of awareness tie us up without any strain at all to the wisdom of being prudent, temperate, just, and considerate. Those virtues also further qualify us in subtle ways so that we begin to see, in turn, that faith, love, and hope also make sense. However, there is no such thing as a sense or a meaning for all to see no matter what. Once one is qualified by changes in oneself one sees what is the case. It is not the case that one is only expressing an opinion or exuding an enthusiasm; one is being so qualified by a deepening and strengthening of one's subjectivity that some objectivities now became apparent, including the truth of Christianity.[4]

Lewis thought it odd that anyone should read poetry with the intent of ascertaining thereby the poet's state of mind. He called that *The Personal Heresy.*[5] Equally, something of the same can be said of Lewis's religious literature. It is not confessional or even a profession of his beliefs. Instead it is at one and the same time argumentative and persuasive. It ought to be noted that Lewis's Christian literature is both sophisticated, in that it supports highly developed thoughts, and popular, in that it appeals to a wide range of readers. He does not achieve the latter by pandering to the notion that he will disclose the secrets of his life or flatter the reader with extravagant spates of experience. On the other hand, it is not as though his literature hides his personal commitments, whether theological, philosophical, or literary.

In any case, my remarks are not designed to tell what Lewis really thought, as if he had a system of thought or an esoteric conviction or some presuppositions that only time and scholarship could reveal. Rather, these pages aim to refocus his litera-

4. To say it this way is to be reminded that Søren A. Kierkegaard also noted this kind of phenomenon in his *Concluding Unscientific Postscript*, passim. Lewis's book referred to here is *Christian Behavior* (1943).

5. And, so, the book with that title. Included are three essays each by Lewis and E. M. W. Tillyard debating whether "to read poetry means to become acquainted with the Poet." (London: Oxford University Press, 1939.)

ture, not to blunt its appeal or to distract the reader from its plain concerns, but to stress what seems again so important and to draw attention to what may be so easily overlooked. This kind of evaluative and critical look may cause a reader to read Lewis with a more heartfelt zest. Therefore, I wish to consider briefly two other components of his authorship that evince the kind of sophistication I have already noted. Lewis wrote most of his strenuously apologetic literature from 1940 through 1947, but *The Weight of Glory* (1949), *Reflections on the Psalms* (1958), *The Four Loves* (1960), *The World's Last Night* (1960), and *Letters to Malcolm* (1963) show us how constant and deep was his preoccupation on these matters. His autobiography, *Surprised by Joy* (1955), made clear that there were other powerful concerns giving shape to his life, not least a life of active teaching of English literature and a rich scholarship to go with it. I wish to allude briefly to that array of activity.

III

Beginning with *The Allegory of Love* in 1936, C. S. Lewis also wrote a dozen or so books of literary criticism and the history of literature. Two volumes of poems (1919 and 1926) never found a major audience, for they were not at all in the manner of the modern poets. There is nothing in them like E. E. Cummings, T. S. Eliot, or Ezra Pound. They have some of the qualities of Yeats—the readability and plainer lines—and surely they share similarities with the great narrative poets of the past and with John Masefield in the present century. Altogether though, this was not the kind of poetry calculated for the readers of *Criterion* (edited by T. S. Eliot) or *Scrutiny* (edited by F. R. Leavis). For those journals seemed often to arbitrate taste for English and American readers, and Lewis was outside their canons. But here again we find him an exceedingly zestful and different kind of author. As his critical powers begin to find their targets, his writings take on a fine polemical edge. Once more he is in a minority, but not crankily so. He seemed to relish *The Allegory of Love* book. It makes a striking case for allegory, claiming that the business of inventing "personae" like "sloth," "joy," "pride," "malice" was necessary in order to describe the psycho-machinations that we all know as our inner life. Lewis's point was that the so-called change of style that led us out of allegory into other kinds of literature also caused us to give up certain kinds of subject matter. The positive side of this book was that it made medieval and Renaissance literature, Spenser, Dante, and numerous others, appear necessary to our self-understanding and not at all anachronistic.

Simultaneously, this book made metaphors and allegories look more like logical necessities than stylistic pirouettes. Furthermore, though the book is a kind of history of literature it does not dismiss the earlier writers as though they were phases through which we have gone. The book does not fit the popular modes of pedagogical historical writing. And there is more, there is the debate with Tillyard in the late thirties in which the popular notion that poetry reveals the character of the poet is summarily dispatched. A little book on Milton in 1942 also makes a case for both epic poetry and Milton, neither exactly a major enthusiasm of the scholarly industry in our time. Though it may be an exaggeration to say it so baldly, it is almost as if Lewis is unable to take seriously the kind of ideological schools that develop in literary criticism. He carried on a spirited attack upon the somewhat vaulted and almost spiritual function of poetry that one finds in I. A. Richards's writings and even in Matthew Arnold of the last century. But against those who want literature to be didactic and more in accord with the age of science (like F. R. Leavis), he has equally strong things to say.

In numerous essays, lectures, and books spanning thirty or more years, Lewis covered a wide range of subjects and authors. The essays are printed now in *Rehabilitation and Other Essays* (1939), *Studies in Medieval and Renaissance Literature* (1966),

Of Other Worlds (1967), and *Selected Literary Essays* (1969). One cannot help noticing that during World War II, when so many people were reduced to helpless inefficiency, Lewis wrote eleven books and numerous of the scholarly articles included in the above. He found little difficulty in conquering his environment. More impressive still is the fact that the major books on literary subjects were so independent of fads and "isms" of the day. In this respect they remind one that his Christian literature is not a part of any school of thought and not riding the crest of any new wave of thought. Thus Lewis's scholarship has to be read almost completely on its own. He is not a "new" critic, not quite the historical sort either, though he has obvious affinities and regard for both. While he is a major historian of literature, he engages in a kind of criticism that stresses the reading of the text.

There is a depth factor here that has to do with the very shape of his thought. This is not easy to characterize, but I will, herewith, by way of anticipating later chapters, note a major feature. Earlier we remarked that Lewis had said something novel about allegory, namely, that that mode of writing was not simply a quirk of earlier authors who because of limitation of culture and period could not do otherwise. Neither was it a propensity or casual trick, voluntary, and one among the several ways that a person might choose to say something. That picture is altogether wrong. Lewis, instead, will have us believe that the subject matter of the *Fairy Queen* and *The Divine Comedy* require allegorical figures in order to be exercised at all. To think allegorically is to encompass a certain "what," not otherwise available. Style and subject matter are so intimately related that they require each other. Therefore, it is not the case that the author can first think of the subject matter in terms and modes that are styleless. It is not as if our minds or our thought-lives are purely conceptual and/or as if our ideas are in a medium of their own. On the contrary, to have the subject matter of those allegories is also to allegorize.

But this account is better stated in the Lewis literature itself. His *Preface to Paradise Lost* makes a similar case for epic and narrative poetry by insisting that there is nothing in the notion of the unchanging human heart to which authors can appeal. But a narrative poem has the advantage of teaching us through its twisting lengths how to realize the myriad possibilities each of us is "on occasion to actualize, all the modes of feeling and thinking through which man has passed."[6] We can do this in an epic because we therein confront all the different things, in highly stylized ways, that each of us can become. Lewis's point is that there is a logic here that is powerful and pervasive. This style issue is like a rule and not a fact to be entertained only as a casual accident.

So through Lewis's long book on *English Literature in the Sixteenth Century* (1954) and his *Experiment in Criticism* (1961), his *Studies in Words* (1960), and even those less polished lectures, *The Discarded Image* (1964) and *Spenser's Images of Life* (1967). Here we do not find only a medley of critical pieces, nor, on the other side, a kind of historical writing that pretends to see development and improvement, or only "influences" and never originality. We could say, I am certain, that Lewis saw all of these things here and there; but the difference is that he did not treat literature as though it had to develop, nor mankind as if it could not be originating, nor, for that matter, styles as if they must be merely imitative. Once more, as on Christian themes, Lewis is singularly free of theories. If he does propose a theory it is a very low-key and small-area hypothesis, by no means a serve-all view. His literary scholarship seems more calculated to improve the sensibility and to enlarge the capacities of the reader than it is to prove a thesis or to indicate a general outlook.

This is to point once more to features of all of Lewis's writ-

6. The Ballard Matthews Lectures, delivered at University College, North Wales (1941) (London: Oxford University Press, 1942), p. 63.

ings that begin to dawn as you read them. Argumentative and rational as they are—they score points and marshal evidence— still they do not hang together in ways that are easy to state. Lewis is not a liberal or conservative theologically, or a romantic or a classicist or a modern-of-whatever-stripe in literary matters. There is a certain shape of thought, a "way" and a "how," of thinking and of addressing a wide variety of issues that saves him from having to construe everything in a school-ish manner. Furthermore, on literature, too, he refuses to think as though every judgment he makes is only an instance of a larger position that he holds; likewise, he does not read authors as if they are victims of their culture, prisoners of their time, nor, contrariwise, as angelic geniuses immune from things earthly. Many factors are, of course, emergent in his discussion and we will not note them here. As with allegory and epic poems, so too with fantasy and stories. The logic of a fairy tale is strict, he says;[7] but his picture is that of differing logics and differing rules, some of them indigenous to an enterprise and some of them field-bound and not otherwise transcendent of their domain. The logic and sense of myths, fantasies, epics, gospels, and allegories are often only to be formed from within their style and subject matter, either and/or both. Thus, no theory about them, no personal critical evaluation, no historical account of their origins, in short, nothing save the involvement appropriate to each is going to help very much.

We shall note further details of this rather striking perception subsequently. There is still more to Lewis's authorship. After all, he wrote more than forty books. I wish in concluding this chapter to note very briefly something about his fiction.

---

7. Note here Lewis's essay, "On Stories," in *Essays Presented to Charles Williams* (London: Oxford University Press, 1947) and reprinted in C. S. Lewis, *Of Other Worlds*, ed. Walter Hooper (New York: Harcourt Brace Jovanovich, 1975), pp. 13ff.

IV

In 1938 Lewis published *Out of the Silent Planet.* It was the
first of three fantasy novels, written almost in the manner of
science fiction. Lewis not only commented to the effect that
style and subject matter were intimately linked, but he discovered this for himself in his long history of fictional writing.[8]
"They are to be tried by their own rules," he says. He also made
the striking claim that stories, science fiction, fantasies, fairy
stories, and plainer kinds of romances simply say best what is
to be said. Once more, too, the form of the story, roughly what
we have been calling the style, also has its own force—"You
find out what the moral is by writing the story."[9] So it was even
with these books.

Perelandra (1943) and *That Hideous Strength* (1945) along
with *Out of the Silent Planet* made a very imposing trio of
interplanetary adventures. But in an almost incidental and casual way all kinds of other concerns are addressed, too. By
choosing to project scenes on another planet, where vices have
no institutional status, where laws are not necessary, where
shame is unknown, one sees in very stark and forbidding fashion what greed, ambition, and self-centeredness finally have
done for our world and its inhabitants. Almost like Aristotle
who said that we could measure motion only by the concept of
the "changeless," so Lewis is also making overt that we cannot
quite judge institutions and people, the world and its planners,
until we get a standard. These novels do that almost by the way.
Their power is also to cause the reader to observe and to articulate the differences between the sinless and the sinful; one

8. Lewis wrote fiction as a very young boy and through most of his life. Cf. his
autobiography, *Surprised by Joy: The Shape of My Early Life* (London: Geoffrey Bles,
1955).

9. These points and the quotation plus more like them can be read in his *Of Other
Worlds,* pp. 3ff., 35–38, 88.

becomes increasingly aware of the mixed proportions that we humans are. Being neither completely vicious nor virtuous, neither sinner nor saint, we have all the more reason given us to seek integrity and truth and to avoid compromising half-measures. A kind of longing for a purer state is born in us by the reading.

What has been said here might make these books sound like mawkish and rather obvious homilies disguised as fiction. They are not. Instead they are exceedingly exciting adventure stories, enjoyable just as they are for the throb of plot and the delightful imagery. However, in accord with Lewis's appreciation of the richness of every person's powers and capacities, he soon is both eliciting in us what is dimly there already and then appealing to it rather richly. I refer to that dim awareness and hope we all have of and for a life everlasting, for a kind of purity and innocence of love and beauty, for being perfect and incredibly sweet and at rest with ourselves, others, and the world. It is as if Lewis's fiction sounds that bell for us. The author dares to think that every one of us is already a living dialectic, a psychomachia, containing striking opposites.

These terms sound outlandishly learned, so an explanation is in order. Lewis thinks very dramatically and gallantly about our mostly mean human lives. Like Dante in *The Divine Comedy,* like Milton in *Paradise Lost* and *Paradise Regained,* like Samuel Johnson in *Rasselas,* and like the whole of the Holy Bible, Lewis thinks that hell and heaven, vice and virtue, wretchedness and happiness, grandeur and degradation are real possibilities for our thought. Such concepts are not alien to our spirits. For the moment, we need not answer the questions: is there a real hell? immortality? damnation? a realm of the Blessed? perfect justice? and the rest. Lewis certainly does not think that these are only ideas in our heads; neither does he hold that these are simply realities to be believed in the way you do invisible electrons or an electrical charge in the wire. For our purposes here it will be enough to note that his starting point is simply that the extreme opposites we have noted are not an imposition upon our thoughts, our wishes, our hopes, and our projects for ourselves and the world. We are, in fact, likely to think and to feel at home with notions of good and evil, light and darkness, and truth and error. These diametric opposites are deeply grounded in us, so that our human dispositions are quite at ease in this kind of frame.

These, then, make up the machinations, the energy and force of our personal lives. Here we have our native psychological equipment to which and by which our lives are advanced, planned, and judged. This is to comment upon the opposites, the conflicting passions that beset us, and to indulge the notion that our lives are like a lived dialogue or a lived dialectic—a mutual confrontation of opposites out of which we have to make some sense. Here, then, is the state of our minds and hearts, a kind of psychomachia, opposites seeking resolution in a successful life.

Lewis will always have us remember that:

> Humanity does not pass through phases as a train passes through stations: being alive, it has the privilege of always moving yet never leaving anything behind.[10]

Therefore, anything germane to the loves, hopes, wants of mankind in one age are probably appropriate now too. The need is always to break through the conventional framework of current thinking that will otherwise keep us shallow and trivial. In his space fiction Lewis shows us how a very shallow kind of mentality develops, oftentimes in universities and public life. Soon an easy and plausible synthesis of science and current attitudes gives it a kind of status. This complicity of ourselves with the thought of the day will often mean that the psychomachia, that dramatic inner life to which we are entitled, will be omitted. We become, instead, by-products of the age and, as John Stuart

10. *The Allegory of Love* (Oxford: Clarendon Press, 1936), p. 1.

Mill said, "made and manufactured" people. Lewis's fiction brings up by fantasy and highly idealized imagination a whole range of possibilities that ordinary discourse and modern times often blur over. The amazing thing is that to have that done for us is also like being reminded of something we have known in a confused way all along. It is, as Cicero said, that, after all, nothing human is actually alien to us.

The fiction and fantasy includes *The Pilgrim's Regress* (1933), *The Great Divorce* (1946), and also *Till We Have Faces* (1956). But each of these is a particular kind of fiction and demands special consideration. Instead, I remark upon *The Chronicles of Narnia,* seven volumes of fairy story, ostensibly for children but also for every adult who has not left his childhood completely behind. These stories, printed separately, began in 1950 with *The Lion, the Witch and the Wardrobe* and ended with *The Last Battle* in 1956. Together they are like a vast descriptive, historical, and geographical account of the strange land of Narnia, that is entered by going through the back of a forbidding closetlike wardrobe that stands in an uninteresting sleeping room. Narnia is full of strange beings, animals of a sort, who talk, who do battle, who suffer, who are subjects of kings and queens. More interestingly, the royalty and the subjects also have to learn to be subjects of Aslan, that magnificent lion. Aslan is not quite tame, and his nature is not totally describable by the conventional rules and precepts. One begins to sense as one reads these stories that, nonetheless, the long-term precepts that span the ages are very serious indeed. The children who undergo these adventures are more or less wise and good, depending upon how the long-term experience on earth has been taught them in relevant maxims. Precepts and maxims might add to human character, but Aslan in Narnia also has a way of precipitating something novel and unpredictable. The animals and the children, too, have to be flexible, for the framework of history and the expected course of events have a way of not being dependable. Therefore, the continuities of kingships, outlooks, and social habits keep breaking up.

The children are clearly enough afraid of this new world while also being attracted to it. One begins to find how odd it is that we all are tempted to believe that the order in which we live is the best possible. Narnia is a very wonderful order and superior to things on earth: but it, too, is flawed. It is finally as if no reigning system of life, no established regime, is enough for beings that have personality. One begins to surmise that the Aslan will finally not let the quarrels of Narnian life ever be resolved only by knowledge or by a blind obedience. Something distinctively appropriate to people and the animals like them is required. It is as though Aslan teaches everybody a new zeal for the quality of his or her life and that doing something with our lives involves knowledge, morals, imagination, and character. Furthermore, how those animals and children live and think determines what they love and finally even know. We get an odd and strange clue, from a land of fantasy, to the importance of the frame of life and mind within which some things become accessible to us.

Once more, the vicissitudes of the Narnians and their neigh-bors give us ample occasions for seeing how morals, tastes, emotions, and thoughts really work. In the land of fantasy, the consequences can be read along with the deeds. We see the promises and the accomplishments within the same context. Future and past, "now" and "then," are differently placed. They do not come in serial fashion as they do in our time-sequence. All the partisanships look bizarre too, and the ideologies begin to seem like very shallow wisdom. We become more prone to see the streak of egotism in all kinds of action and the triviality of identifying wisdom by the latest ideas. Increasing one's own moral stature in a certain way begins to look like the royal road to immortality if not to plain survival and durability.

Maybe this makes the Narnia *Chronicles* sound heavy and didactic. They are not. Instead Lewis has the delightful and sane notion that good literature cannot be written save to be enjoyed and tasted just for itself. In this sense a good writer simply presents something, in this case a few stories, and the reader has to take it from there. Lewis did not try to make them propagandistic or a sly form of religious apologetic. I think it fair to say that he succeeds. But there is still that matter of the shape of our common human thought.

In brief, then, Lewis's literature shows us something without quite arguing it. Probably it is a mistake to state it in the fashion we already have, for then some readers will think that assimilating this theme will suffice for their response to reading Lewis himself. That will amount to missing the aim altogether!

Lewis would have it that literature actually creates thoughts in us; it is not only about thoughts, it causes them to exist. It is as if literature is not a description of emotions; rather, it so describes states of affairs that the ordinate emotions are invested in us. Literature is not about existence so much as it is an addition to it.[11] It gives us experiences, feelings, moral pangs, wishes, hopes that we have never had. The issue here is not the detail (that will come later) but the broad morphology of his literature. Whether in his Christian works, his criticism, or his novels something fundamental is being done that marks him off. It is as if his disinterested understanding, exercised in the "about" mood in his criticism, coheres with his interested and persuasive writing about morals and Christianity. And what governs both of these is illustrated and beautifully evinced in his novels, both the science fiction and the *Chronicles.* Altogether it adds up to something like this. Literature is not a disguised theory, nor an implied didacticism. Instead, it communicates in such a way that, when successful, it creates new capabilities and capacities, powers and a kind of roominess in the human personality. One becomes susceptible to new competencies, new functions, new pathos and possibilities.

Once this is seen, then Lewis's insistence upon a theory-free criticism of literature begins to make sense, for there is a func-

11. "Fairy Stories . . . ," in *Of Other Worlds,* p. 38.

tion upon which one can judge the poem and novel without invoking a hidden thing or agenda. It becomes feasible to construe a kind of Christian literature, including the Bible and his own writings, as being sometimes free of an embedded theological position. Lewis's stance does not have to look like a cheap anti-intellectualism; instead it bespeaks another kind of even deeper understanding. All of this supposes that the form and structure of Lewis's thought is part of a very deep and extensive kind of rationalism. It is as if his work has made manifest how variegated God's creation really is. For people are delightfully complex, and their reflective capacities match and make that complexity.

The Christian literature does not merely propose a doctrine to be believed nor a policy to be espoused. If that were the only way Christianity could be advanced among us, its appeal would be only to those who could think big ideas and entertain vast plans. Instead, Lewis addresses all of us where we are, faltering and stumbling, uncertain of what we should do or be. We are all open to a promise, poised for a great happiness, and already eligible for the sweeping away of the shadows of guilt and disappointment. Maybe our moral life, bumbling as it might have been, might have given us enough sorrow about ourselves to seek a way out. Maybe, too, we have hoped a little and discovered the vanity of much of our wishing. Christianity deepens those misgivings about ourselves into repentance and that fitful expectation into an encompassing hope. These things are, again, capabilities that have to be articulated and then strengthened in us. For Lewis this is the way Christian literature, even Jesus' teaching and early discipleship, ought to work. So he does it. The novels bear the same point for all of us. There we see the psychomachia happening in others. And critical literature never lets us forget how literature can really work in us. All of his work seems to have a common shape.

In the ensuing chapters, I want to address some issues that will make plainer these elementary matters. The first concerns will be with theories and the role of literature.

TWO

About Theories and Literature

MOST LEARNED PEOPLE in the twentieth century are used to radical uncertainties. We are inclined to believe, in virtue of the easiest sort of compliance with the spirit of the day, that any one of a dozen incompatible philosophies that we have got used to might be true. On the other hand, because we have so many theories, philosophies, and theologies, we are sometimes prone to think they are all about equal and that nothing much can be said that will confirm one over another. Logic and facts "seem" to be on all sides or none, as the case may be; and "relativism" and "indifference" look the better part of sophisticated wisdom.

Lewis was a part of Oxford when this opulence of beliefs and theories was already a feature. He, too, felt the kind of skepticism that comes from knowing the variety of views and from everlastingly looking at a range of alternatives. Obviously there are ways out of the debilitating indecisiveness, and some of them are desperate indeed. For one thing, one can simply settle for the options and remain undecided until evidence comes in. Lewis heard people recommend such an attitude on the grounds that it was scientific in contrast to being dogmatic, antiscientific, Christian, or willful.[1] This attitude is also supposed to be eminently rational, for it suggests that reality itself has to be waited upon to confirm one's views.

Lewis is not willing to define this attitude as the most mature and obviously rational one. His reasoning seems to be subtle, but is not for that reason too difficult to understand. What is wrong with all of this, Lewis suggests, is that views of life, theologies, and general outlooks (call them philosophies for the lack of a better term) are also put into this kind of context. Such theses are likened to theories, to points of view, to hypotheses, and then they become the kind of material that pedagogues and professors can talk about. For if everything must be talked about, if the issues of life must be expatiated upon endlessly in lectures, pedagogical books, outlines, and seminars, then all the issues, theological, literary, philosophical, also take on the shape that is demanded by such modes of discourse. Soon everything becomes a position, a point of view, a hypothesis or a problem; for these are the coin of the academic realm.

Few authors of our time have been as at home in a university as C. S. Lewis. He seemed to be made for Oxford and Cambridge; and it looks now in retrospect as if he graced the podium far beyond expectations and youthful promise. But few authors and pedagogues have kept their intimate thought-life as independent of that context. He became a Christian, for one thing, when the Oxford world was scarcely conducive to it; he gave up idealism as a synthetic philosophy to interpret all other philosophies without becoming a schoolish antimetaphysician or an obvious positivist: he went his own way, not picking and choosing literary "isms." Rather, he forged a conception of what theories and people were such that the logic of indecision, of relativism, of countless incompatibles was bypassed altogether.

1. "On Obstinacy in Belief," in *The World's Last Night* (New York: Harcourt, Brace and World, 1960), pp. 13–31.

It was as if theories were not the fundamental subject matter, either in great literature, for making a life virtuous, or for becoming a Christian. He says flatly: "On my view the theories are not themselves the thing you're asked to accept." Here he is talking about Christianity and the difficulty of deciding to become a Christian: but the view applies very widely. It is as if a set of theological theories, all of them disputable and highly conjectural, do not have to be resolved before you can believe as a Christian. Religious belief does not consist in deciding in favor of one rather than the other. The theologies do something else altogether. So do the esthetic theories about literary matters. It is not as if the development of poetic taste depends upon deciding which kind of poetry is superior or whether the "stuff" of the poem was worth communicating.[2] Here the differences abound. "Rationality," as commonly projected, suggests that we cannot proceed to liking, to taking pleasure in, a real esthetic experience until we have decided these weighty matters. We cannot decide unless we arbitrarily join a school or become an advocate for whatever the cause. The point is that joining up seems like an irrational move that is required before one can become moral, Christian, literary, or just plainly responsible. The terms are already defined that way. It is precisely those terms that Lewis repudiates and just how, we will note in subsequent sections of this chapter.

II

The mistake at the heart of all of this can be stated in a categorical and straightforward manner, but it cannot be understood and exercised quite so simply. Lewis has a character in a novel say that one cannot study human beings, but that one can get to know them. In several other places he distinguishes

2. "Donne and Love Poetry," in *Selected Literary Essays,* ed. Walter Hooper (Cambridge: Cambridge University Press, 1969), p. 121.

sharply between *connaître*, which is getting to know by becoming another self, sharing the feeling, pathos, and hope, and *savoir*, which is knowledge in the "about" mood, theories and views, laws and hypotheses.[3] In poetry circles, the thought seems to be that there are experts, the critics, who know poetry the way chemists know chemistry. In psychology there seem to be experts on humankind, who will now know humanity under general laws and who will clarify the kinds and judge the successes. The demand seems plausible enough—that there be experts everywhere and that the experts produce the general knowledge that we all seem to need. Lewis, on the contrary, can give no credence to the idea of the expert in areas like religion, morals, and esthetics.

The experts are those who propose some general rule under which the instance must fit. Not only is it difficult if not impossible to define such an expert, but the difficulties multiply as one entertains the general laws. About poetry there are schools, historicists, "new critics," "expressionists" and hosts of others. Their pronouncements are numbing when entertained in any number, yet not to do the latter smacks of one-sidedness and partiality.[4] About people there are behaviorists, Jungians and Freudians, materialists and spiritualists, all willing to propose, if not laws, then rules and very general theses about what human nature is. One could add, of course, the social theorists, those who see literature and people as economically determined, the anthropological theorists and historians of taste. The point is, obviously, that Lewis is not repudiating the quest for knowledge nor the insatiable curiosity that wants to know. His thesis is a logical one.

It is, briefly, that general laws do not and cannot explain

3. E.g., in *An Experiment in Criticism* (Cambridge: Cambridge University Press, 1961), p. 139. Again note his *Of Other Worlds* and *The Personal Heresy*.

4. Note especially *The Personal Heresy*, pp. 116–17. Also, "On Criticism," in *Of Other Worlds*.

human behavior. People are not knowable, except in the breach and in exceptional cases, in such a manner. Rather, the rule is that everyday explanation is the model. You understand me if I say that I did not do as I promised because I thought, upon later reflection, that it would be wrong. Here one gives a moral reason for conduct and it has a kind of ad hoc character to it. We ask why someone did something and we are told because she wanted to. We usually understand this reasoning. Desire for something explains the behavior in this case, while aversion to the person or situation explains it in another. Soon we are all caught up in a web of everyday explanation by which we understand human actions. And it is this texture of understanding that we gradually become acquainted with as we experience more and more and live with attention and sagacity.

It is precisely such a loose and nonmethodical kind of explanation that has seemed so precarious and so chancy, especially as certain kinds of learning have prospered. We all seem to yearn for a kind of science of human nature wherein the action of human beings will be subsumed under general laws and be made as predictable as the movements of the planets and the permutations of the genetic components. It looks plausible to suggest that if the chemistry of the body, if the genetics of our physiology, if the color of the babies' eyes are covered by a general hypothesis, why cannot the whole of humankind be brought under general laws? Then morals, esthetics, and religion would also be explained.

Lewis would say, I believe, that to couch the human scene in such terms can produce nothing more than we already have. The "Great Myth" suggests that the evolution of learning is finally going to bring humankind under its sway and that everything human—art, religion, poetry, and ethics—will very soon be founded on facts and be describable totally the way we describe the behavior of inanimate things and animals under encompassing formulae and rules. Lewis thinks he can describe the funeral of that myth, but I think he is wrong on that. For the myth of scientific explanation and the notion that this "must" be extended to everything human is far more inveterate and deep-seated than his account suggests.[5] He would have it that the popular confidences are rooted in a theory of progress and necessary development and that these are being repudiated. Maybe so; but the notion of this kind of explanation constituting the only true knowledge of people goes on unabated.

The salient factor is that no general laws are ever proposed which are verifiable and significantly predictable. Mostly they are either so loosely related to human life that they permit alternatives and are, hence, undecidable on the grounds proposed, or they are so general as not to be informative. Lewis sees this predicament of the learned, this perpetual impasse, as a consequence of a typically modern logical mistake. Knowledge of human nature cannot be in the form of general laws at all. Theories here are out of order. But there is such a thing as getting to know human beings. There is such a thing as getting to know poetry very well too—and both of these without theories. So, too, with getting to know oneself, but more of that later.

There is no substitute for general wisdom and a tough health of mind. In poetry one must know one's language exceedingly well and certainly have "a wide experience of poetry." This is not knowledge in the conveyable and rather standardized sense. It is the kind we refer to when we say that a wise person is knowledgeable about human beings and human history. There is such a thing as becoming very wise here and full of understanding. Finally this range of qualifications is what is also needed to make a person a great literary critic; but it is also what is needed to make a person a competent judge of human behavior. "Understanding" in this instance is not a theory nor a catena of them; instead it is an achieved capacity of the

5. Note his "The Funeral of a Great Myth," in *Christian Reflections,* ed. Walter Hooper (Grand Rapids, Mich.: Eerdmans, 1967), pp. 82–94.

individual, in virtue of which the person is enabled and empowered to see, to discern, to know, when another is lying, when the ad hoc explanation makes sense, when the stated wish was the actual motivation, and when the asserted love was pretense and when it was not.

Literature is not dependent, then, upon theories. More properly, literature does not teach theories in the guise of fantasy and fiction. Neither is it, therefore, only an emotional expression of the life of the age or the idiosyncrasies of the individual author. Literature is produced in a myriad of circumstances and for an indefinitely large number of purposes. An unsuspected consequence of the reading of literature is that it enlarges that everyday capacity for explanation that we already command. By thinking and feeling with persons in literary contexts, not so much the authors themselves, but with the fictional characters and by the help of the individual poetic lines, we extend pathos, passion, desire, wishes, and we become, ideally, more competent ourselves. Literature adds to reality, it does not simply describe it. It enriches the necessary competencies that daily life requires and provides; and in this respect, it irrigates the deserts that our lives have already become.

The point, however, is many-sided. Actually much of this pseudoscience and bad theory makes us suspicious of the emotions, the desires, the wishes that we use to explain ourselves in everyday life. Therefore, that ordinary kind of explanation is thought not to explain at all. Instead, it is as if the emotions, the wishes, and the hopes that supposedly are to explain something are themselves now made the object of an explanation. They are, indeed, sometimes not the explanation, and we are occasionally mistaken about them. Lewis, however, does not want to think all thoughts are tainted at the source because some of them are. Clearly some thoughts are rationalizations and disguises for something else about which we might not be clear. I can confess to being offended by my colleague's overt patriotism when actually I detest the man himself. In cases like that I may be tricked by my own emotional involvement and misstate the issues.

Right here Lewis sounds the warning about "Bulverism," which is his epithet for the practice of using a general theory about thoughts being tainted at the source to give an account of all thoughts, thereby relieving one of the necessity of checking out each thought-content in turn. So, too, with emotions. If emotions are only indexes to the way an individual feels, then that theory obviates the hard work of relating the fear or the hate to its object, whatever it happens to be.[6] This, again, is why Lewis thinks that one cannot have a theory at all telling you what emotions, passions, faiths, and morals are supposed to mean. A theory cannot do that, for there is no general meaning and no general law has anything to which it could correspond. The very shape and form of a thought is such that with a thought we do explain. But we cannot then go on to explain the thought. Explanation must come to an end. Something like this has to be said of emotions, too. It is only the exceptional thought that can be thus explained and then usually because it is out of order and perhaps inappropriately engendered and defended. Then its irrationality requires the explanation. One cannot explain rationality.

Lewis says:

> But you cannot go on "explaining away" forever: you will find that you have explained explanation itself away. You cannot go on "seeing through" things forever. The whole point of seeing through something is to see something through it. . . . To "see through" all things is the same as not to see.[7]

6. Note the essay by that title in *God in the Dock,* ed. Walter Hooper (Grand Rapids, Mich.: Eerdmans, 1970), pp. 271–78.

7. *The Abolition of Man* (New York: Macmillan, 1947), p. 50. Lewis also says: "No one can, in any ordinary sense, meet or experience a photon, a sound wave or the unconscious. . . . We are not even, in the last resort, absolutely sure that such things exist. They are constructs, thing assumed to account for our experience, but never to be experienced themselves." *God in the Dock,* p. 249.

The fundamental matter to which all of this applies is that no general law will do anything but add confusion. If a person says that the waterfall is sublime, it sounds as though the person is commenting about the waterfall. Lewis quotes the authority's general law diagnosis:

> Actually . . . he was not making a remark about the waterfall, but a remark about his own feelings. . . . This confusion is continually present in language as we use it. We appear to be saying something very important about something: and actually we are saying something about our own feelings.[8]

Lewis's point is not simply that this particular theory is mistaken, but that no theory about emotion can ever substitute for the ad hoc and widely diversified range of competencies that are required to think, talk, and feel in ways that such a use of language proposes. There is no correct theory, because no theory at all can suffice. Something radically different is needed. The ad hoc mode of explaining must not be abrogated because there are "caused" thoughts and inordinate emotions that deceive us. We must become more competent and that means more sensitive, discriminating, more apt with descriptions, and more acute in feeling. Then only will we be able to see whether the waterfall is truly sublime, the man actually hateful, and the situation very sinister. Emotion-words require competencies that are rare. Acquiring those competencies is something that a rich life can supply. But a literary and esthetic experience can do it too.

III

There are other ways that Lewis keeps himself out of the grip of theories. Once more it is important to remember that Lewis is not saying that a theoretical interest is absurd or that knowledge is useless, nor, contrariwise, that poetry is superior to

8. *The Abolition of Man,* p. 2.

science and intuition better than discursive reasoning. He does not project his thought in those comfortable and cursory ways. Nonetheless what he has to say is both appropriate to a long-standing tradition and yet original, because it is so seldom remembered, or articulated with clarity, or made vivid by imaginative reflection and illustration. He manages all of these.

There are ways that we come to know what is the case other than by theories, beliefs, hypotheses, and general laws. In short, this is what Lewis learned for himself and not via a theory, and this assurance gave him a somewhat jaunty and casual air toward the making of theories in some areas. Already we have noted that Lewis has a character in *That Hideous Strength* suggest that we cannot study human beings, i.e., make them a subject of science, but we can get to know them. There are, patently, all kinds of small logical issues that can be raised about such a matter. Lewis does not raise them, and I choose not to do so on his behalf. We will make his case by marking another kind of concern that we alluded to above.

If one comes to trust the somewhat crabbed notion that all knowing and all assurances must be via theories or laws (what is called sometimes the idea that knowledge must be "propositional"), then we have in Lewis's way of speaking, "savoir," or what Bertrand Russell called "knowledge by description." As far as I can tell, C. S. Lewis never disparaged the zest for such, be it about whatever you please. Sometimes Lewis talks about knowing something "by acquaintance," therein invoking the paralleling expression made familiar again by Russell. But he does not suppose the range of issues that Russell does, and he uses that expression without incorporating the whole theory that the philosopher had enjoined upon his readers.[9] Nor does Lewis think that scientists ought to be intuitive, or, with Berg-

9. Readers who are not familiar with this distinction between knowledge "by description" and "by acquaintance" or with Bertrand Russell's views might turn to his *Problems of Philosophy* (Home University Library, many editions). Also, it will be well to remember that Lewis began his studies in philosophy and that he even tutored in the subject at Oxford.

son, that we ought to supplement one method with another. Such is not his point at all.

Instead it is precisely that in these difficult areas, usually covered by literature, by philosophy, by theology, and even by psychology, where the stakes are so very high and yet the theories are so inconclusive, matters are being wrongly addressed. Here we are often concerned with the nature of reality, with what man is, with the beautiful and the good. Seemingly there are issues that are momentous, with which, as Samuel Johnson notes, we are concerned perpetually and "by necessity," whereas in most other arenas we are curious only "by chance."[10] Yet we get here the incompatible views and unsettleable issues. I have already noted that Lewis thinks wisdom is available to us, but it cannot be written down as one more thing. We have to become wise, and this kind of wisdom is a mode of character, actually a virtue. But more must now be said.

For the logic is altogether wrong. Ethics, religion, metaphysics, and even esthetic concerns soon lead us nowadays also to theories. Lewis does not believe that any such pursuits, becoming moral or a Christian, knowing reality, or enjoying a poem or a painting, are intrinsically and essentially a matter, respectively, of believing in a theory of the good, a Christology, a metaphysical scheme, or of knowing the beautiful and finding it instanced in this poem or this object. Yet he knows that we can and must be certain about what reality is, who we are, and what is good, true, beautiful, and just. To couch these issues in familiar theory-form is to guarantee, if one stays alert, an everlasting postponement of decision; or a premature foreclosure and a naïve pronouncement if we stay intellectually innocent; or a truncated ideology that occasions arbitrariness or proffers factors that are extrinsic.

Literature here suggests a way out of our perplexity. Not

10. S. Johnson, "Life of Milton," in *Lives of the Poets* (London: Oxford University Press, World Classics, 1973), vol. I., esp. pp. 72–73.

because the theories of literary figures are more subtle and diffused. Nor is it because literary figures are all geniuses and more able to decide; nor are they Prometheans and originals and hence no longer subject to rules. A great piece of literature, for example, *The Divine Comedy*, shows us a great piece of human life. But it is not an encyclopedia; nor only a summary of the thirteenth-century mind, a map of Scholasticism; nor an index to a past culture. One can read it, obviously, with many interests. A sprawling allegorical epic like that can yield in a surprising number of ways. Lewis would also have us read it remembering and relishing the extravaganza that it is. That long poem limns and fits not only Dante, but it also limns and fits a potentiality, maybe the actuality, that is the reader. Those magnificent lines were natural and powerful, flexible and efficacious, for Dante himself. They belong to him and were of his very "stuff."

A mistaken view—again a theory—was proposed by Tillyard and was denied with vehemence, yet good humor, by Lewis. That view said that great literature was an expression of the "psyche" of the poet, that it finally could only be understood, if and when one knew what the poet, for example, Dante, meant and intended. Lewis is at pains to deny this particular view. Of course, something of this kind has been said by R. G. Collingwood, by Benedetto Croce, the Italian philosopher, and numerous critics since. Lewis does not deny that a line in a poem is germane and appropriate to the poet, otherwise he could not quite have managed to write it. But the perfection of a poem as well as the perfection of an art piece is that the idiosyncrasies of the artist are finally not what count. A piece of music is like a language—its units and parts, the words and the sequences of notes—do not get their meaning only from the particular user. They already "mean," they are part of a living tradition and a lively language, and they are put to new uses only because they are already meaningful.

A poet like any other artist does what no one else can do, but he does not, therefore, express his own personality.[11] He or she does indeed start with a particularized consciousness, odd though it might be; but the artistic outcome is an arrangement, either of words, as with poets, or sounds, as with musicians, or other material, as with painters and sculptures, such that a kind of public experience becomes possible. The artistic creation simply "is" something. It is a construction admittedly, and its "stuff" comes out of real life and actual people. But the synthesis is new, and it may picture a familiar scene or not as one chooses. The point is that the artist's mind is not being pictured.

The experiences one has in such moments of reading, seeing, and hearing are not merely reproductive and copies of earlier experience. Lewis would have us remember that a new kind of consciousness is being made in us as we thus enjoy the poem or esthetic object. We are not only establishing contact with a great mind, that of the artist. Instead, great poetry, again Dante's, for example, tells us not so much about Dante, or even Beatrice or Virgil, as it projects via a host of circumstances and personages what are phases of our common human nature, detached from historical conditions, which might happen. Whether they have happened or not is often irrelevant to the value of the poem. The point is, rather, that the poem makes them possible and conceivable by putting them into sense-making words and contexts. We begin by sharing the poet's words and consciousness, his way of seeing the world and people. That consciousness cannot be only idiosyncratic. The public words and the public contexts the poet describes soon make that consciousness no longer the prerogative of any one individual. The better the artist, the sooner we are away from the oblique and the personal. The poetry stands after a while almost without the poet. Obviously it needed the poet in order to be said and the

11. Again, note *The Personal Heresy* (London: Oxford University Press, 1939), pp. 26–27. Also, *An Experiment in Criticism* (Cambridge, Cambridge University Press, 1965), pp. 74–87.

reader in order to be experienced.

What we now have, however, is enough to give us pause. We begin a poem sharing in all probability the poet's oddnesses; but if the poem really works for us we begin to apprehend something else. The poet (but also the musician and the painter) is constantly dependent upon the public fund of words. He also shares the "sensibilia" and their names—summer, night, wood, stars, gust, air—and all of these are part of the funded capital, "the bank on which he draws his cheques."[12] The words, parts, items of experience were not peculiar to the poet—they are in the public domain and belong to all in the same tradition. The arrangement he gives them, or his experiencing them in a distinctive manner, is initially his own. But the poem is not a piece of art if it is only autobiographical. It is artful only if the items, sensibilia and words, objects and thoughts, are united into a new synthesis for all of us; then it becomes an artistic creation. We now can see not the poet but people and the world differently. We attend and intend the world differently.

This is also to learn what the world itself is. It is not poets who matter except as the authors of poems. The great poetry of the world stands precisely because there is a world—people and things, tradition and history—that is not created by the poet but is apprehended by the experience and the consciousness that a poem sustains. We see "through" the poem; what we see is not the poet but whatever the poem happens to talk about. Just at this point, however, it is important not to let other general theories of what the world is intervene. Many of us are, in all likelihood, rather amateur materialists, mostly because we have imbibed a theory about the world being made up of atoms, matter, and strange forces. This kind of popularized scientific outlook, probably too gross for specific theory, tends to make us think that poetry is only subjective and a matter of a point of view.

12. *The Personal Heresy,* p. 19.

Lewis is again after us here for our easy assimilation of theories. Theory tells us that poetry and fiction, indeed most art, are only a kind of creative indulgence, part of the graces of human life and never a part of the substance. Or it would make the arts look only like a decoration and never a part of the serious cognitive enterprise. Science would seem to be the truly cognitive substance that tells us what is what. Poetry and the arts would give us the adiaphora and the pleasantries. No wonder, too, that some estheticians want to say that the arts are only emotive and expressive, but important insofar as emotion and expression are part of the human scene. Once more a theory tells us what art and poetry mean.

In such a state of affairs, there are those who want to blur the lines between science and poetry, those who want to talk about two cultures, and those who want to claim that there is an emotive, hence poetic, aspect in all of science and a cognitive, hence scientific side, to all of poetry. Poetry may give us the hunches, the anticipations of nature, the disguised poetic factors. Against all of this Lewis generously polemicizes.

A simpler consideration is suggested in what we have already noted. Literature—the allegories, myths, fairy tales, epics, lyrics, novels—has its limits, its rules, and its proprieties. It cannot be just anything. It never is sheer creation and totally and radically new. It is always an arrangement of what is already there, but it is sometimes a new arrangement. Literature is not blind and fortuitous. Never is it simply a random concatenation. It fits something and is something. People use it, but to their pleasure and not to footnote their religion, favorite philosophy, or the reigning politics. The work of art, the poem, says something, but it also is an object, carefully contrived and sometimes complex. It delivers us from our mediocrity and self-limitations—it, as an object, says something; but it forces us to attitudes, feelings, emotions, and passions that other human beings have had, that the world itself allows and, indeed, requires.

It is as if one receives more than one seeks. The very shape of poetry, as well as the arts, forces us out of our personalistic slant on things. It forces us, too, out of the grip of theories and hypotheses, though it does not exactly substitute for them. However, a deepened grasp of what literature can do for us will probably mitigate our tendency to take hypotheses and laws for more than they ever can be. They do not give us reality. The temptation to think so is part of a philosophical and meta-scientific bias, not itself a piece of science. The force of literature is to strengthen those tendencies we already recognize as a matter of common sense and an endowment of everyday life and experience. For we all know that there are differences between the everyday world and the world as described by the sciences. The table in the room is solid and reliable. Described by atomic theory it seems to be full of spaces and a mass of moving particles. Which is it "really"?

The difficulty most of us have in assimilating the sciences does not inhere in finding out all kinds of details. These can be assimilated without too much travail. The crunch comes when we begin to ask, "But is science the truth?" Surely we want to say Yes; but do we want to say that the table is not solid, the body not impenetrable, the fear nothing but a brain-wave? If we are persons of common sense, we refuse to confuse ourselves; and we think peacefully enough about tables, bodies, and emotions as the situation demands. We do not deny the scientific account for the sake of everyday acknowledgment, nor displace the everyday way of reckoning because we have a new scientific account.

The difficulty comes because we think "real" and "true" and other such big words must be univocal and definitive for all contexts and circumstances. So, then, we say: "What is the world really?" Commonsense would say what it always has said. The words "world," "real," "true," "sense," "nature," "life," have long histories, and they have spawned many differing concepts. [13] A sense, common to all kinds of people, has

13. Note here the sections in Lewis's surprising book *Studies in Words* (Cambridge: Cambridge University Press, 1960), where some of these concepts are explored.

been ensconced in some of these words, and they serve again as a bank upon which we draw. But surely, there is no right in a popular fashion, or for that matter a science, or a religious or a peculiar philosophical outlook, of determining once and for all the meaning of "real" or "true." That is what happens if a theory, philosophical or otherwise, begins to legislate.

Common sense usually keeps such legislation at bay. Literature and the arts do now have a particular strength in this respect. Just as we noted that a kind of wisdom of life makes our ad hoc explanations better and more reliable, worth attending to, rather than replacing them by general laws, so poetry and literature, almost inadvertently and seldom by design, strengthen common-sense capacities. They give substance to the logic and morphology, to the very grammar, of our everyday discourse and thought.

Therefore, no theory about art can tell us what the art means. This we have to ascertain by becoming resilient and tasteful, delighted and competent. A great poem will add to our stature, by feeding not just our pleasures but our zest for them and our capacity to have them. There is, thus, no shortcut. And so, too, with reality. A metaphysical theory cannot provide it. Instead the very order and grammar of literature is what Lewis seems to have discovered; and that manner, and that mode, in which it works to enlarge our seeing, hearing, feeling, and knowing shows us both what our human nature is like and what the world itself is. Then one needs no theory; instead the literature takes care of itself by becoming efficacious. One cannot anticipate its outcome, nor predict its judgments. People are in a world like that, and, in turn, people are like that too. Once one gets the hang of oneself and of the world one is in, that transmutes into a way of thinking that is wise. And literature can provide that dawning recognition.

IV

The organon for reality and truth is not quite the hypothesis nor wholly the metaphysical theorem. Again, we must remember that when we think so, we are led almost immediately to the question, "Which metaphysics?" or "Which theology?" or "Which psychology?" There are too many, and the evidence is both too much and too inconclusive. This is where literature and ordinary living must be considered in imaginative detail.

The woman, Orual, who is unwittingly that dark and terrifying Ungit, "ugly in body and spirit," is a major subject in Lewis's *Till We Have Faces.* The novel is a taxing book to read, both because it requires such an imaginative effort, and because it says things that are unfamiliar and which indict the reader when understanding dawns. On the imaginative side, the work, like all of Lewis's fiction, fuses the fanciful, the mythical, and the marvelous, on the one hand, with the major themes of Aristotle and Plato and Western moral pedagogy and even Christianity, on the other. This is an uncommon synthesis. Most Christian writers and ethical theorists have invariably stressed the differentia, not the similarities. Lewis's point is not that ordinary. He takes with great seriousness the picture of human potency and capacity. Any person is, in principle, capable of realizing what others have become, especially in matters of esthetics, morals, attitude, passion, and even faith. Thus there are exceedingly good people who seem to be morally discerning even though they live in contexts that do not solicit the same; so, too, there are, almost by nature, Christianlike people who live in a pagan society. These are the *anima naturaliter Christiana.* Once more even the myths of ancient Greece and Rome suppose some development and clarification of personality, and that kind of achievement is reduplicable in any society and time. Greece and Rome threw light on contemporary life and morals. By imaginatively exploiting the myths and fancies, and not by describing them negatively as prescientific or subsuming them as typical of the childhood of the race, Lewis synthesizes the early and the late, the marvelous and the scientific.[14]

Thus with Orual, who suffers the agonies of ugliness and isolation from all that she loves. Gradually she comes to realize, amid conflicts and heartfelt tensions, that the gods cannot meet humans until humans have faces. Humans cannot be enveloped in pretense and be veiled by indecision and contrary wishes. The clouding of the person is a consequence of moral-like ineptitudes. Thus Orual learns: "You, woman shall know yourself and your work."[15] Orual is not a symbol any more than are the animals in *The Chronicles of Narnia.* Instead, Lewis himself insists that she is an "instance," a "case" of "human affection in its natural condition, true, tender, suffering, but in the long run tyrannically possessive." Her story stands on its own right. The better it is, and the less of the author there is in it, the sooner will one note "the close parallel to what is probably happening at this moment in at least five families in your home town."[16]

It is not as though we need Jung's archetypes to explain how ancient Greece can throw light over our daily life. Whether we are all in the grip of unconscious archetypical thoughts and images might be an interesting conjecture. It might even be used to explain how some themes become perennial in world literature and art. But for Lewis this is like an aside and one that cannot be made anything but a plausible guess. There is, how-

14. Note here Lewis's criticism of Frazer's *Golden Bough,* in "The Grand Miracle," *God in the Dock,* pp. 80–89, and, by contrast, his treatment of myths in "Williams and the Arthuriad," in *Arthurian Torso* by Charles Williams and C. S. Lewis. This one-volume edition includes also *Taleissin through Logres, The Region of the Summer Stars* (Grand Rapids, Mich.: Eerdmans, 1974), pp. 275ff.

15. *Till We Have Faces* (New York: Harcourt, Brace and World, 1957) p. 282.

16. These remarks are excerpted from Lewis's letter to Professor Clyde Kilby (February 10, 1957), in *Letters of C. S. Lewis,* ed. W. H. Lewis (New York: Harcourt, Brace and World, 1966), pp. 273–74.

ever, another way to claim some of the ground and that is to learn to read the myths and stories. Then one will discover potentialities in oneself and achieve a kind of clarity—acquire a face, even a character—that will be first hand. Orual even says that if she practiced philosophy, not the way Fox did in the story by presenting clear rationalistic schemes, but in the manner of Socrates, then she would change her soul from an ugly one into a fair one.

Now we turn to two related deliberations that are pertinent. We have already said something about a piece of literature being simply an object. As an object it also begins to create a new consciousness, when properly read, of the world and oneself. Literature is not objective quite the way a scientific description is. In fact, it gives us acquaintanceship with people and situations, not theories about them. Literature does that. It gets us used to people; it presents them as subjects and not as objects. To say that a piece of art or literature is an object is to say that it is objective about a mode of human subjectivity that its author may or may not share. The reader begins to share the life of the literature; he even has actual emotions and pathos, as he reads. Bad literature describes emotions; good literature so presents situations and contexts that the appropriate emotion happens in the reader.

The first deliberation about this is raised by Lewis in his debate with Tillyard when he asks whose consciousness is this that is being engendered. He will not admit that the author's is being simply transposed to the reader. And the reader usually feels that the myth or the story is not a matter of knowing only the poet's mind. Instead Lewis would remind us that our own logic is "a participation in a cosmic Logos."[17] And I wish to do justice herewith to that theme. Lewis, it must be remembered, is far from being an idealist philosopher, who would be prone to speak generously about pan-logical schemes. He does talk

17. *Surprised by Joy*, p. 209.

about reason and logic in a way that conveys the notion that he holds a philosophical view, but rather surreptitiously. I do not think he does.

Instead, literature, like everyday life itself, brings one to a kind of objectivity and grip upon the world that is better than one's idiosyncratic grip. That consciousness we then share, that reality we then acknowledge, that logic we then encounter—all these (they merge into one) are part of a logic that is cosmic. This is to remark upon what Ludwig Wittgenstein called a "grammar," a way that things fall together and the pattern of rules which articulate the way things are.[18] It is as if we soon can enjoy poetry without the poet. More tellingly, even, it is as though a vast sweep of literature begins to portray more than it or the poet says. The idiomatic and nonartificial language articulates a form in the world that we then begin to share. So, too, is it with common sense in everyday life.

Correlative to this, though, is the other thought, the second deliberation, lingering at the edge of all that we have been saying. It is not finally that theories and points of view can teach us that much or say that much for us. Finally it is a person who has to become the knower. And what a carefully managed daily life can do, so also a literature can materially aid. We can become knowers, and "we" can be subjects who know. In this context, then, "knowing" is not a matter of having a large store of facts or a panoply of laws at one's behest. Becoming a knower here supposes a readiness to see, a facility to size things up, a quickness to understand. One becomes knowing and accommodating to the states of affairs, not simply well informed or erudite.

Reality for Lewis is not something that can be summarized in a theory. One can have capacities for it. Instead of assuming

18. Lewis, too, uses the word "grammar" in an analogous way when he has Dimble say: "But that's only the grammar of virtue" in *That Hideous Strength* (London: The Bodley Head, 1969), p. 461.

with a kind of vague intellectual tradition that one must start with names and particulars ("all the different kinds of trees, but not about 'trees' ") and finally get to the reality of things in very general remarks and with very general concepts, Lewis suggests almost the opposite. General laws and universal concepts get one off in abstractions and away from particulars. So he says in a letter:

> In their final stage they are admirably clear but one is so far away from real things that they really say nothing. . . . Compare "Our Father which art in Heaven" with "The supreme being transcends space and time." . . . the first really "means" something, really represents a concrete experience in the minds of those who use it; the second is mere dexterous playing with counters, and once a man has learnt the rule he can go on that way for two volumes without really using the words tc refer to any concrete fact at all. . . .[19]

It would take more effort to know via that first quotation, however, than the second. And a true knower has to equip himself or herself, transform and sensitize abilities so that words like those will become something like spectacles to look through, not look at. It is as if then a logic of a situation, of a state of affairs, is finally being broached. And we are no longer simply wallowing in points of views and perspectives. Once we become accustomed to no longer looking at the literature, or for that matter, at the facts around us, always trying to discern their hidden law or their portent, we are free to let the world and poems do their more fundamental job upon us. Then the logic of the world, the morphology of things the way they are, can really be received. It is that receptivity that counts here.

By always thinking big and forgetting oneself, one can easily get the reputation of being concerned with transcendent and massive "real" issues. By calling all such concerns a preoccupa-

19. A letter to W. H. Lewis (January 17, 1932). In *Letters of C. S. Lewis,* p. 147.

tion with reality, one has an almost invulnerable position. Perhaps this is why Screwtape, that infernally wise teacher of tempters, recommends this stratagem so highly: "the fatal habit of attending to universal issues and withdrawing his attention from the stream of immediate sense experience."[20] More particularly, by always assimilating theories and using literature and everyday life to create them for us, we place all emphasis upon knowledge and little upon the knower. Knowledge, oddly, will fail and utterly pass away, but the apostle Paul will have us remember that charity will not. The latter cannot be written down, and the remark can only suggest that a person of charity will never be vanquished.

Throughout his writings, Lewis puts the emphasis in the same sort of way. The truly wise person will finally be Orual in *Till We Have Faces,* Ransom in the fantasy pieces, even Peter in the *Chronicles,* none of them schoolish metaphysicians. But they are exceedingly well taught. None of them thinks within points of view. Just as self-sacrifice and love for others are not standpoints or religious doctrines, so being wise and understanding are not either. These are ways we must live. These require a tempered spirit and a chastened and well-honed intelligence, not less but more. Eutace, a somewhat stubborn boy, says (in *The Voyage of the Dawn Treader,* chapter XIV): "In our world, a star is a huge ball of flaming gas." He is told by a wiser head: "Even in your world, my son, that is not what a star is, but only what it is made of." Stars are also wonderful, awesome, and fearful. Stars and moon are many things, and the somewhat inchoate-appearing logic of ordinary discourse and everyday life requires appreciation and sensitivity, susceptibilities and impressionability, like that of the psalmist, of Dante, of myth-makers, as well as scientists.

It is as if the logic of our world is too big for a theory. It requires, instead, rational, deeply humanized and deeply

20. *The Screwtape Letters* (New York: Macmillan, 1943), p. 12.

modified subjects. It is in them, in contrast to the depraved, the immoral, and the thoughtless, that the grammar of the world begins to take shape. Again we are perhaps close to something called "common" but not "vulgar." This is a sense of things, a sense for things and how they cohere. The great literature of the world represents more than it ever says. It is not only a tradition to be cherished and a debt to be acknowledged in sentimental ways. After a while the wise man is the person in whom the truth and nature of things is received. This sense is not only invented and imposed, as a kind of positivism would have it. This sense is a kind of logic or grammar, and by sharing it we know where we fit and who we are. This fittingness is a good part of our wisdom, available to all who pay the price that cultivation, moral and esthetic, literary and cognitive, finally exacts.

THREE

Concerning the Virtues

SURELY WE HAVE not done justice to Lewis as a student and critic of poetry and literature if we omit all consideration of his own poetry. His *Dymer* (1926) is a myth, and Lewis says that it is "the story of a man who, on some mysterious bride, begets a monster: which monster, as soon as it has killed its father, becomes a god."[1] This long romantic story has an epic quality about it, and its heavily rhymed lines seem exceedingly appropriate to the immensity of the predicaments, the sheer size of Dymer's wish, and the magnitude and force of the apparent psychological issues. There are echoes here of Malory, of Milton and Spenser, but scarcely anything of a troubling unconscious, of tortured social aims, or the fretfulness of the modern man, which he so singularly abhors. He seems not to be troubled the way T. S. Eliot, D. H. Lawrence, or Ezra Pound were. Nor did he ever find murky symbols, blurred images, "free verse," and the modern sensibility really worth the effort. He

---

1. This remark is included in Lewis's notes to the 1950 reprinting of *Dymer*. Now conveniently printed in C. S. Lewis, *Narrative Poems,* ed. Walter Hooper (New York: Harcourt Brace Jovanovich, 1969), p. 3.

46

was at home in an older literary context.

Once more there is that curious blend of high imagination and a feel for the specific facts. And there are no intervening theoretical schemes mediating between the two. It is as though the poem itself is the actual means of achieving a heightened awareness of what the world is and also so strengthening the inner man that a more precise definition of our common human nature becomes possible too. "To read Spenser," Lewis says, "is to grow in mental health." And this brings us again to consider the literature he liked best. For the knights, dwarfs, dragons, and sorcerers of *The Fairy Queen,* and the sparkling heroes and fantastic glades, forests and natural scenes, for all of this, Lewis has a deep appreciation in others and a facility in creating, if not in his poetry, then surely in his novels. There is something in Lewis almost like Spenser in another respect. When commenting upon Spenser's proclivity for the doctrines of the new-Platonists, he asks how Spenser could call himself a Christian and believe in them. But then he says:

> ... The whole school of thought to which Spenser belonged felt that in the long run "everything" must be reconcilable. There was no belief, however pagan or bizarre it might seem, that could not be accommodated somehow, if only it were rightly understood. The other answer is that Spenser may not have intended the doctrines as articles of belief at all.[2]

More important to our purpose here is the plain fact that Lewis always liked that kind of literature, long narratives and idealized epics, where the simple certainties between right and wrong, good and bad, worthy and unworthy, purposeful and aimless are clearly celebrated and where the beauty makes one ache and the tragedy has real consequences. It is not the human scene itself that makes much sense, so Lewis does not ask

2. *Spenser's Images of Life,* ed. Alastair Fowler (Cambridge: Cambridge University Press, 1967), p. 59.

literature to be realistic and actualistic in ways that are ordinary. Naturalism as a literary mode, Lewis thought, was a concession to an untrained and very average perception. The popular literature and the blunted mentality which takes this to be reality—and James Joyce's *Ulysses* with its fragmented psychological hero—these were an altogether too plain reminder of what such a world is like. This world is familiar enough, but finally in Lewis's view it is not the norm by which to test a literature. Another kind of "seeing" and "hearing" is open to all of us, and this is what the great literature helps bring about. It is as if there is finally an everlasting truth and an indefeasible grasp of things that is open to anyone who is both logical and romantic, sensitive and cogent.

More particularly, all of Lewis's writings seem to me to assume a fundamental ethic, a clear and certain delineation of moral value, that is available for all, in turn, to know.[3] The poems already are documents to Lewis on behalf of such a view; but more, they are, when read with care, the means of clarifying both the reader and the objective scene so that a moral vision can take place. All of this, however, makes Lewis sound like the arch instance of someone who is using literature rather than properly receiving it. I will therefore qualify the foregoing by saying that Lewis had apparently understood something about ethics itself that gave him assurances, where most of the twentieth-century moral theory only saw a morass of ethical theories. Just what that is, I will note in the succeeding sections of this chapter. But think again what Lewis says about *The Fairy Queen:*

> It is, as we say, a comment on life. But it is still more a celebration of life: of order, fertility, spontaneity, and jocundity. It is, if you like, Spenser's Hymn to Life. Perhaps this is why *The Fairy Queen* never loses a reader it has once gained. . . . Once

3. I owe a great deal to Nevill Coghill's essay, "The Approach to English," in *Light on C. S. Lewis* (New York: Harcourt, Brace and World, 1965).

you have become an inhabitant of its world, being tired of it is like being tired of London, or of life.[4]

II

Lewis tells us: "Really great moral teachers never do introduce new moralities: it's quacks and cranks who do that."[5] Furthermore he insists that there never has been and never will be "a radically new judgement of value" in the course of world history.

> The human mind has no more power of inventing a new value than of imagining a new primary colour, or, indeed, of creating a new sun and a new sky for it to move in.[6]

All of this sounds dogmatic and assertive, almost as if Lewis is unaware of the plaintively touching predicament of modern man where ethical systems are plural, where there is so much to choose between and yet so little to inform one choice rather than another. The dramatic issue of the so-called contemporary is, furthermore, that moral systems are thought to be subjective and modes of adaptation, useful perhaps but never true.

We are faced here with a situation that demands an explanation. Lewis is not easy to explain; he surely is not just a stubborn Protestant who will insist that his conviction is God's will. He is not so archaic that everything contemporary is alien to him. Besides, his certainty on moral fundamentals is too many-sided and too detailed to be merely a stray bit of Aristotelianism or a lapse in taste and thought. He discerns this kind of attitude in Spenser, in Dante, in Aristotle, and a host of others besides. More than that, the conviction about an elemental and plain moral teaching is ineradicable and crucial. It is so deep that it seems always to have been a discovery, never a point of view,

4. *Spenser's Images of Life*, p. 140.
5. *Christian Behavior* (New York: Macmillan, 1943), p. 13.
6. *The Abolition of Man*, p. 29.

and never one possible system among other systems. This is why it enters so naturally into his interplanetary novels and supplies the matrix and measure for all worlds, for Narnia, Venus, ancient Greece, and his England.

No wonder then that Lewis likened himself in this respect to Dr. Johnson, who thought that on moral matters ". . . men more frequently require to be reminded than informed." And he refused to believe that all moral teachings were intellectually equal or that, he, on the other hand, was advancing one. But just why this obtains is not altogether clear.

Part of the reason for this lies in what he takes morals to be. Contrary to modern opinion and practice, he does not slip into any kind of modernist view at all. One kind of modernism is the sort which thinks that what is missing is always the right policy. Because we get used to thinking about whole nations and "modern man" and starving millions, we are prone to believe all individual morals are something of the past. Today, we tend to concur, we need an up-to-date moral outlook that will tell us what the good is for all of mankind, as if it follows as a matter of course that then we can do it. With science made almost institutional and government using legislation as an instrument for social goals, it seems that a morally insightful policy is the principal need. Furthermore, we are all modernists like this, not because we think but because we do not. Lewis resisted this panacealike mentality and all the nostrums bedecked in moral garments—the welfare state, the growth of science, the popularization of education, socialism, and even the pictures of nations united to prevent war. Somehow all of these lacked what he wanted more than anything else, namely, a bright and infectious felicity that would catch all of us up in an intelligent and deep passion.

To Lewis there is no doubt that most of us illustrate the fact that our character is a quiet consequence of what we think. If we allow ourselves to be caught up in the popular concern about solving all the social problems of the day, we will soon come to believe that poverty, ignorance, and social deprivation are the worst evils. When we drift along, have no grand feelings, and merely respond, then we are prone to trim down our desires and wishes too. We begin to fit in and a moral mediocrity sets in. It is as if our intelligence gets unhinged, and we take the truancy of disposition and the random character of ethical planning as the best that we can do. Lewis calls a halt to all of that, although few people actually did as much as Lewis did to relieve poverty and suffering. Nevill Coghill, his long-time friend, and others seemed to be awed by his kindnesses and by the fact that he gave most of his money from his popular books away as fast as it came in. But, unlike most of us, he did not impose his own will upon others as if it were a general will, nor make the maxim governing his behavior into a general law. Morals did not work that way. Nor did he finally come to believe that what he, thereby, did was the highest good, just because it was within the reach of social policy.

That is why the vogue for social planning and policy-making is so dangerous. We are easily victimized by an abstract picture of goodness, a kind of fatal idea of a common way of life that will be necessary for all to reach the standard. Lewis would have it that God did not make any two saints, nations, angels, blades of grass, or ordinary people quite the same. And, furthermore, the spark in all of us has to be nursed and brought to flame. But how shall this be?

Here is where Lewis remembers the virtues. Almost as old as the race itself, the language about virtues lies almost forgotten among us. Of course it is written large for us by Aristotle and Plato, both of whom discerned pivotal moral excellences that moralists ever since have thought were cardinal and almost like hinges upon which the door of life would swing. These excellences are wisdom, temperance, justice, and courage. Centuries later, Christian thinkers added three more, so-called theological virtues, faith, hope, and love. For a long while, too, the list of seven virtues was thought to include those crucial kinds

of personality formations that would enable one to live a happy
and useful kind of life. It is interesting to note that Lewis brings
all of this to the fore again. He even does it in a popular series
of broadcast talks on the subject of Christianity.[7]

The virtues do not predict behavior, nor do they formal-
ize and standardize human beings. On the contrary, they
lead to a life in which genuine individuality is encouraged.
For when courageousness and fortitude become a habit—
and all virtues have to be customary rather than single oc-
currences—the individual becomes strengthened and qualified to do all sorts of things that were otherwise inconceiv-
able. An entire range of behavior becomes open to such a
person, and so, too, with the other virtues. They are en-
abling, disposing, and authorizing. Such an ethically sensi-
tized person no longer simply fulfills a rule or law, except as
a part of moral pedagogy or where circumstances require it.
The moral life becomes the arena where adventure, individuality, and tasks are continually brought together. There is
rather little being done in the abstract or in general terms;
the sense-making activity is a life moving resolutely into
novelties, guarded by dispositions that are temperate, courageous, hopeful, just, and, eventually, even wise.

Contrary to the opinion of our day, Lewis says flatly that the
"cardinal" virtues are recognized by all civilized people but the
"theological" are, as a rule, known only by Christians. I think
it proper to Lewis's literature also to remark that he does not
seem to think that morals thus conceived and Christianity are
always in tension. Protestant teachers have often used the apostle Paul's warnings about the inability of the law to secure
rightness before God to cover also the virtues. The synthesis,
therefore, between the natural and supernatural virtues, that
Thomas Aquinas and Thomas Hooker made, was and is often
criticized as Christianly unsound. Lewis will not see the issues

---

7. *Christian Behavior.* See esp. chaps. II and X–XII.

that way. And this is not because he is antibiblical or anti-Protestant, and pro-Catholic and pro-Anglican.

It is, rather, that he again frees himself from having always to construe every kind of moral action as if it involved assenting to an ethical theory or even to the general idea, "law." We "construe" a sentence in a grammatical fashion if the sentence, "She caught the frog" is diagnosed as "she" is the subject, "caught the frog" is the predicate, "frog" is the direct object. In a similar fashion, we tend to conceive of all human situations as if they, too, can be "construed," and moral theory-talk becomes a way of doing that. Our desire for general talk and the assurances we get from using formal concepts probably account for the quickness with which we do this. Think for a moment about the person who is trustworthy and honest, perhaps also favored with a confidence and hope in God. How tempting it is to "construe" such a person as "believing in God" or "believing in the general good" and leave things there. Ethicists after a while lose touch with the specific likings, animosities, disappointments, griefs, odd wants that persuade this person that he had better keep himself trustworthy or else he could not make sense of much of anything. So it goes—each person is also host to a dramatic range of circumstances which he assesses, with striking differences being exemplified. If there is any construal going on, it probably is not—at least in every case —via a generalized sense of duty, a necessary imperative, or a policy for a better society. These large-scale considerations are not the instrumentalities at all.

Moral culture as Lewis outlines it is not a matter of fitting particulars to universals, or subsuming instances in one's personal life to general laws; instead, it involves the actual development of wants and desires, hopes and cares, and then also the capacities to judge them in a variety of ways. It is as if every person is being outfitted and made ready for the dangerous world and a world in which the qualities of the individual begin to count very much indeed. These qualities come very slowly and eventually become either virtues or vices. The complexity of the virtues becomes clear here too. To take one example, courage is not, after all has been seen with some clarity, only "one" among several virtues. Rather, it is the very form itself of any and every virtue at its testing point. A person who was chaste or trustworthy only when there were no dangers or temptations involved would not miss courage very much. Add the testing context and it takes the habit of a courageous response even to keep one's chastity.[8] Through all of this, however, it is evident that morality cannot finally be "construed." We cannot understand it save by a manner appropriate to what it is. This means that the virtues begin to frame a life that makes sense. And knowing how these virtues (think of them again as habitual ways of being disposed) make a life is to understand that life. But the available and knowable stuff here are all the concrete and everyday factors, longings, appetites, aversions, expectations, trusts, confidences, which if they are put together very well, make the person reliable, whole, and a living synthesis.

In addition, the virtues simply recommend themselves. They need no case made for them at all. They are not part of a point of view nor components in a hypothesis. Whether one is attracted to them or not depends upon the way one's emotions, wants, and feelings have been trained. More than this, it also depends upon what one has done with himself or herself. Therefore, "courage" is not an option at all; for there is no conceivable person for whom "cowardice" would be a viable choice. Being cowardly is always like a lapse, whereas being courageous is a genuine achievement. So, too, with temperance. No one can make sense out of intemperance except to describe it further as folly and absurd. This is to show again that those cardinal virtues are the very ground of being rational.

Moreover, it is not true that one simply assents to the idea

8. *The Screwtape Letters*, p. 148.

that temperance or courage is good. That again would make it appear superficially intellectual. The fact is that one eventually simply likes being temperate, takes pleasure in being courageous, finds contentment in practicing wisdom, and enjoys justice. More than this, one is at peace with oneself and becomes, not a conflict, but a synthesis.

There is for Lewis no thought that morality must always be a dutiful imposition upon one's nature. Sometimes it might be, but that depends upon the kind of person one might have become or the state of one's moral development. Unlike Kant, the great moralist of the eighteenth century, who distrusted the empirical self with all of its desires and impulses, and who thought that inclination and duty would invariably be opposed, Lewis felt that both the moral and the Christian ways of life would lead to a working accommodation of the two. Besides, moral cultivation also means that one grows more rational and sees more clearly what is the case. Prospering in the virtues also means that one learns more and more. Becoming moral is a subtle kind of education within itself. "For what you see and hear depends a good deal on where you are standing: it also depends on what sort of person you are."[9] What comes in view are more and more specifics, not general schemes. These specifics are loved, wanted, and enjoyed. They make their own claims upon us.

III

One of the most familiar distinctions in the modern intellectual world is that between facts and values. It is so widely espoused that hardly anyone thinks *to* it anymore; on the contrary, it has become almost axiomatic, so that most people think *from* it. For Lewis, the distinction is surely a deeply misleading one, and once more it is his whole literature that renders it for

9. *The Magician's Nephew* (New York: Collier Books, 1970), p. 125.

the most part useless and inappropriate. Insofar as there is any argument about the distinction it must overlap Lewis's rejections of naturalisms and materialisms, and these are noted in several diverse contexts. However, the novel *That Hideous Strength* juxtaposes Dimble and Ransom against that average kind of naturalistic mentality that grows up in the modern universities. Frost, who is the intellectual impressario in Belbury, speaks for the facts:

> When the so-called struggle for existence is seen simply as an actuarial theorem we have, in Waddington's words, "a concept as unemotional as a definite integral" and the emotion disappears. With it disappears that preposterous idea of an external standard of value which the emotion produced. . . . When you have attained real objectivity you will recognize not "some" motives but "all" motives as merely animal, subjective epiphenomena. . . . And that is why a systematic training in objectivity must be given to you. Its purpose is to eliminate from your mind one by one the things you have hitherto regarded as grounds for action. It is like killing a nerve. That whole system of instinctive preferences, whatever ethical, aesthetic or logical disguise they wear, is to be simply destroyed.[10]

The purpose at Belbury, where Frost reigns supreme, is to forge a new kind of efficient institution that will directly and without the delays of persuasion, build new people and a society. The intellectuals there are surprising, like many we already know. As the novel makes clear, Belbury is a place where the general drift of a very powerful modern point of view is no longer merely talk—it is now policy. (Had Lewis lived through the 1960s he could have as easily noted that many of the young people who were tearing down the things of which they did not approve were also effecting only what their teachers had been

10. *That Hideous Strength,* pp. 365–66. In another context, Lewis refers to the limitation in a certain kind of explanation on the grounds of its basis being "this particular way of working." Cf. "Miracles," *God in the Dock,* p. 36.

saying but not doing anything about.) Everybody at this new place is supposed to stand only by the facts, brutish, bare, and given. By choosing to define facts as they do—and that is the point, they "choose" so to define them—then all preferences, desires, and emotions are declared to be subjective, and offensive for that very reason.

Lewis knew full well the offense that the intellectuals took at notions of subjectivity. His *Abolition of Man* argues that those who say that poetry is only subjective or that emotions are only feelings in the subject and never a feature of the thing being judged ("the fire is dangerous," "the situation is hopeful"), are also prone to dismiss values, emotions, and passion. Surely he is right. Because facts are ostensibly discovered and values are made only by subjects, the latter are both dismissible and, by the same token, capable of being arbitrarily imposed. And if there are no standards by which we are governed, then who is to govern becomes all-important. The professors who have discovered this state of affairs also want to be masters, rather than victims, of it.

The tragedy at Belbury is that Frost has to destroy everybody else's subjectivity so that his alone governs. Somehow he wants to believe that by saying that all value is subjective he at least has made a claim compatible with the facts. But he has only fooled himself. Facts looked hard and changeless to him and had only one kind of verifiable and positive knowledge to go with them. But values were different. Here we had the conflicts and opinions, at least so he thought, and little or no agreement. What Frost overlooked is exactly what Lewis thinks all of us invariably do. Because we share a kind of positivism or a kind of naturalism, really mostly an attitude and, in some cases, only a theory, we tend to postulate this realm of neutral and given facts. Better still we could say that this is a game we have all been taught to play. Lewis describes that game in numerous contexts and the game typically assigns religious dogmas, poetry, morals and emotion to the value side and hence, subjectivity.[11] Then these altogether share triviality, no evidential claims, and reflect their shallow hold upon us. Furthermore, by assenting to the idea that the other game is fundamental and plain, options and opinions begin to multiply and an arbitrary, crazy, and irresponsible madness begins to grow up. People invent, or try to, new moralities and new theologies just as if that is now required. Against this Lewis pleads the massive unanimity of the practical everyday reasoning of ordinary people.

Another form of the fact-value bifurcation is found when one begins to say that the education in facts is value-free, whereas the education in values is optional and a matter for family, churches, and interested groups. Still another is to insist that value is a matter of being obliged, ostensibly this feeling being a very comprehensive "sense of obligation" brought to the neutral world of facts by the rational subject. Two sets of laws are then envisioned: one, the general laws of explanation; the other, laws of a legislative and evaluative sort.

On these issues Lewis does not couch his misgivings in typically philosophical ways. Once again he does not propose another theory; but this is a way in which his imaginative works and literary diatribes constitute a very wide look around. In this wider perspective, no longer truncated by a theory of what reality or morals are, a kind of dawning recognition begins to occur. It dramatically occurs to Mark Studdock in the novel noted when he begins to reflect hard upon who and what he is. For with this young descriptive social scientist, it had never occurred to him to think about morals. Oddly enough, there was not anything like a moral experience either. There was, at least, no sudden onslaught of an obligation, no decision to mount a value, no conclusion to the effect that facts are not

11. Lewis criticizes those literary critics who think that they can do without "the grammar of conduct," this serious and "unyielding core," even to make sense of comedies, irony, and the great tragedies. See "A Note on Jane Austen," in *Selected Literary Essays,* pp. 184–85; also, note the "Poison of Subjectivism," in *Christian Reflections,* pp. 72–82.

enough. All the conventionalities of popular ethical discourse were bypassed.

In the insane world of Belbury, where Mark now lives, the context had the effect of making him aware of the opposite. Just as absence makes affection well up and sorrow teaches the loveliness of everyday companionship, so suddenly he became aware of something commonsensical and "normal" about which he simply had not thought. Soon he was aware of how massive and solid it all was. His thought wandered to his neglected wife, Jane; it got mixed up with things he liked and loved, fried eggs, soap, sunlight, and the noisy rooks cawing away. The point: "He was not thinking in moral terms at all; or else (what is much the same thing) he was having his first deeply moral experience."[12] Suddenly it occurred to him that he was really preferring the ordinary and the normal; and if that led him away from the so-called scientific point of view, then the latter had to go.

Right here, though, the plainness of Lewis's literature makes us think it is very subtle. We are so accustomed to highly contrived accounts of the moral life and to having our thoughts everlastingly described as objective if we are having to do with facts and subjective if we are considering values, that we can scarcely gather in the drift of his ideas. Not for a moment is Lewis denying that there is a world around us, that in an obvious sense, it is there to be known and described. On the other hand, he is not denying that people are people, that we are, typically, the ones who have the ideas, the emotions, the purposes. In this sense, we are subjects, not objects. The difference is that Lewis will not concur with the notion that the language of science is uniquely objective. Furthermore, he rejects categorically the view that there is only one literal language that reproduces the structures of the world. There is no norm in one kind of language that is particularly factual and

12. *That Hideous Strength,* p. 369–70.

"about" the world, whereas all other ways of speaking are more or less subjective.

This must be said with great care. One finds in his pages very little about "symbolic" language in contrast to "literal" and nothing whatsoever to suggest that mathematical symbolism is necessarily more appropriate than everyday discourse at telling you what is what. Lewis is not one to deny the advantage of technical language for its given purposes; but he denies the philosophical notion that we have already called "positivism," which suggests a singular kind of discourse that is factual. Partly this is so because Lewis knows both the ambiguity of the concept "fact" and the many ways in which words work. In *The Allegory of Love* he notes that allegorical figures are better able to represent "pride," "sin," and other emotions, virtues, and psychological factors that our daily life helps us to isolate; and that if we give up allegory we have no way of talking about such matters. We usually change the subject.

The same kind of thing can be said about logic itself where the whole tissue of supposedly the most analytically precise schematism turns out to be metaphorical. Once more, metaphors are not always or only stylistically pleasant; how else could we describe conclusions "following" from premises, the premises "containing" the conclusion, the "point" of the argument, and numerous others? Therefore, there is no one way to describe anything. There are ways for this purpose and that.

Thus there prove to be many ways of speaking about what is. Just as we noted earlier that poets are also describing something and not exclusively inventing and contriving, so their language is not subjective and symbolic. It, too, refers; and it may require a good deal of transformation of an individual's consciousness to get him to refer in the same way. Lewis would have it, however, that doing morality is not a special activity requiring a special sense or a particular skill. In one sense, there are no experts because morality is not a craft at all, and it is not like carpentry or being a linguist. Rather, moral factors are everywhere and morality is not a special field. This is not to say that certain qualifications do not enter in and help create the certainties and arrest the skepticism. The issues inhere in how the individual addresses the whole of his life. Just because all persons are equally subject to moral order, just as we all are to the physical order, there is a fundamental equality in the moral life. We do not need moral impressarios, such as Belbury spawned, to rule the majority. Instead, people are of one kind, no matter whether on this planet or another, if they are considered as subjects to one context of moral reality.

The fact-value distinction is, therefore, abrogated. Seeing facts is not an exclusive prerogative of any one discipline. The entire range of kinds of seeing, hearing, thinking is subject to qualification. It is Lewis's notion that how we see, hear, and think depends upon attitudes and large-scale conceptions of the logic of our disciplines. It is that logic that Lewis's literature seeks to change. And he does not offer a theory of the good. He shows us repeatedly in his novels how a kind of moral certitude is finally achieved. He sends us back to our fathers, mothers, nurses, poets, sages, and lawgivers. The dignity he ascribes to all of us is exceedingly flattering. He wants us to remember that they, in turn, are offering us only a secondary account. We already possess, as it were, the original manuscript, our lives, and our roles in the drama of life. The tissue of life around us, when taken with seriousness, is already a moral order. We have to become its qualified readers. Every reading is qualified. The world has no single character and it must be understood in a variety of ways. To read it with everything moral and esthetic abstracted out is to make it a caricature of itself; to read it with these factors admitted is to see the very logic and sense of the world.

IV

C. S. Lewis's thought is so different because it is not neatly separated into kinds and compartments. He is a moralist without a definitive moral thesis, a theologian without being a schoolish type, a critic without having quite a critical theory. More positively, everything he wrote is pervaded by his sense of the drama of man's sublime situation. A dark enigma dogs all the bright planning and prospecting upon the future; a strangeness insinuates that the outcome of all stratagems and promises always will be different from the expectations. Lewis is not prone to say that is the case only because the variables are so many; instead, it is that goodness and justice are at the heart of things, yet are missing from the hearts of people. He dares a diagnosis in the almost desperate belief that it is not the lack of wit and intelligence that will mean the resolution of human desperation, but the coincidence of human will with the goodness that is already knowable. Lewis conjectures that most of us are like the magicians of old, who thought the principal issue was how to subdue reality to the wishes of men. Nowadays this is done by applied science and politics, which become the instrumentalities of all of the new ethics. In contrast, Lewis finds the heart of ethics, the principal problem, to conform the soul to reality itself. Clearly, ethics is not, all the same, a singular activity. Our mode of conforming to reality is to become disciplined, knowledgeable and, finally, virtuous.[13]

Lewis's orientation is radically different from the moral philosophy that we know in both continental European circles and recent Anglo-American philosophical contexts. It is tempting to use his own strong avowal of a "natural law" thesis to lump him with some kind of moral objectivism, with Hartmann and other metaphysicians on behalf of morals. That slight resemblance does not do justice to Lewis as a thinker, even though it has to be admitted that, in the heat of controversy, he does say extraordinarily strong things about the objectivity of law, both moral and scientific. However, I do not think those can be enlarged into more familiar kinds of moral (or philosophy of science) theory, if one remembers what we have said about his

13. Remarks to this effect can be read in *The Abolition of Man*, chap. III.

intention not to let a moral, poetical, or religious theory ever cut off the genuine discovery and drama of everyday life, of savoring the very lines of the poem, of worshiping God Almighty. It was this range of activities that Lewis took with seriousness, this "how," which made a statement of the "what" gratuitous. Furthermore, it was in the prosecution of this "how" that one would find the "what" in a multitude of satisfying ways. Again, it was the satisfaction he was seeking to cultivate.

Lewis's moral reflections do not seem to me to be an exercise in archaism or a mere flaunting of the old in the face of the new. He relishes Dr. Johnson, Aristotle, and others who discuss the virtues and the vices. But the shape of his thought is not exclusively made by his long-standing preferences. Somewhere in his determined reading, letter-writing, and endless conversations, an important discovery was made. It was as if his own thought had to be shaped to that discovery thereafter. I have no single incident to cite and no epochal hour to record. But, in the numerous letters, hundreds of them, in the early poems and essays, on through all of the later writings, an accommodation was being made.[14] Instead of Lewis bearing in his own person the vicissitudes of the theoreticians' battles, I think he made another kind of discovery independent of the theorists. It is comparable to Wittgenstein's noting that there is a grammar of thought and language which is not just one more permutation on theorymaking. So, it seems to me that Lewis had noted the manner and mode of human life in such detail, and not only noted it, but reconstituted these modes in his letters and in his stories. The upshot was not another theory.

Wittgenstein thought that the person who understood the

14. I can only cite here two long series of letters, which span fifty years of give and take, plus numerous individual letters. These were read by me over a period of weeks in the Duke Humphrey Library at Oxford University. They are the letters to Arthur Greeves and Owen Barfield.

grammar of a given linguistic usage would be freed thereby from the necessity of forming another theory. The grammar would be "known," not by a theory but, rather, in the practical ways in which we put a sentence together. We simply do it; our linguistic behavior is ruled in practice without the rule being cited. Lewis's originality and force as a moral thinker does not rest on his contributions to the moral theories of our time. He did not enter those debates, except to get at attitudes that often lay behind them and gave them a popular currency that was undeserved. He did not, seemingly, read Gilbert Ryle or Ludwig Wittgenstein, and certainly he shared little with modern Oxford moral philosophy.[15] Very remarkably, what Lewis has done, without the help of Wittgenstein, is something very close in kind. We cannot call him Kierkegaardian either, though there is a resemblance there too. He has seen the close connections between what people see and know and how they live. The "what" and the "how" are related in a variety of ways.

Lewis saw very clearly that the framing of a life was the moral task. There was no abstract principle and no alien obligation that could be thrown into that task. Every person had to be energized and stimulated into doing that for himself. It was as though the individual had to find the means within his own personality to do just that. His wishes, emotions, and aspirations, these and more, were the instrumentations by which a life was mannered and formed. So, no general concept, no theory about the good, would ever be anything but a substitute, and a poor one at that. The grammar of morals was plain as Lewis thought about himself and others. His own extraordinary self-perspicuity gave him, I believe, a running start on piecing that

15. It must be noted, however, that Lewis was president of the Oxford Socratic Club from 1942 until 1954; that he was a "prime mover" in getting philosophers to debate especially the pros and cons of the Christian religion; that he responded in print to H. H. Price and Miss G. E. M. Anscombe, both well-known philosophers. Note here "The Founding of the Oxford Socratic Club" and the succeeding pages in C. S. Lewis, *God in the Dock*, pp. 126–46.

shape of morality together. It got larger as his knowledge of others became extensive and as his literary competencies grew too.

Certainly it is not inappropriate to remark on how inexhaustible a mine he had in the language of conversation. The learned can often mask their lives in impressive talk that is not quite their own and within which they do not actually negotiate their lives. That language is not "of" anything that is their own, but usually belongs to a third party. Lewis, on the other hand, had a great enthusiasm for conversation and with a wide variety of people. This is why his pages are so full of surprises. For example, the ludicrous tramp in *That Hideous Strength,* who is mistaken by the intelligentsia at Belbury for an emissary from a previous existence, is no highbrow and his English is, by certain rules, fractured. "Gor', blimey. Couldn't have believed it. It's a knock-out. A fair knock-out."[16] But amid those ejaculative bits of conversation, a kind of sanity looms up; and even his confessed unabashed love for cheese sandwiches begins to give a shape to the notion of what people actually are. Amid the wildness created by the pseudo-learning, Mark Studdock finds his grip on reality returning through the tramp's conversation, odd as it is. It, at least, had gusto and an earthy sense. So, too, with the cabby's vernacular in *The Magician's Nephew.* It brings a realistic order to things just when everything else gets out of kilter.[17]

The fact that Lewis appreciated so much the conversational flow of a variety of people is important. Here the language begins to be a part of a form of life and it is not about it. In the cases above, to understand their talk is like reaching back into the qualities of the lives of the speakers, for their talk is an intimate part of their lives. Once more Lewis is at ease with the strong speech and metaphorical wit that one finds in the every-

16. *That Hideous Strength,* p. 408.
17. Ibid., pp. 92ff.

day concourse. This is why, too, his own paragraphs are a sort of splendid conversation. We can now add the additional point that Lewis's literature tends not to need an artificial learned language to convey moral worth. His skill in creating a rich idiomatic language that is in the mood "of" morals is why he is a moral teacher without having to urge a normative theory upon the reader. Moreover, he knew not only moral judgments but also the kinds of mouths and lives in which they would be found. His books create, almost as Kierkegaard did, the living variety of paradigms. This is what would be required, obviously enough, if a form of life were important.

The remaining fact to be remarked upon is that Lewis chooses not to make a case for morals. We have noted this already. But a further consideration is due. Kierkegaard, the nineteenth-century thinker, said there were at least two kinds of communication. In one, and familiar, instance we communicate a bit of knowledge to someone else. That person understands, assents to what we have said, then that is the end of the matter. The other kind of communication Kierkegaard called "indirect," and he thought it peculiarly required in morals and religion. In the latter instances, we are also being taught to become something different. Here the requirements are new capabilities, new capacities altogether. In this case, what one writer can do for another, his or her reader, is primarily to engender that kind of concern and self-regard in which the capability will grow up naturally and quickly.

Once more without apparent debt to Kierkegaard, Lewis has made this kind of accommodation to people and to the very structure of moral life. I think it just to say that Lewis himself had made that kind of long-term adaptation to moral fact without the juxtaposition of outside help. He did himself what we have been noting all along as something suggested by his literature. That literature itself, not only the novels, but most of it, becomes the very logical mapping of the way morality inheres in the race. The whole thing has a shape and grammar about it that shows us, and does not only tell us, as we read. If it told us too often it would become propagandistic and a matter of inept and inappropriate persuasion. Soon a theory would be emerging—perhaps a normative one; but it never quite does emerge. Yet the force of the whole is unmistakable.

We now become aware of an integral component in Lewis's thought. For his works, especially the novels, have a way of creating a kind of longing for innocence, for purity, for humility, candor, and contentment. This is part of that indirect communication at which he is so good. He is causing us to create for ourselves all kinds of these aptitudes and propensities we simply did not have before. With the aid of these, in turn, we become capable of forming our own lives anew. So, too, with religious things. It is not as if Lewis invades our privacy with his alien moral authority. Neither does he condition us, as was done in Belbury where objectivity was destroyed. Rather, Lewis finds that morality is not directly imparted. Only its occasion can be created by another, and that is what Lewis's literature becomes. The morality finally has to be achieved by a sensibility that is enabled, empowered, and qualified. All of that can be done only indirectly. Once more, one can see the wisdom in Lewis's mode of writing. Wisdom has to be read off the whole shape of his thought and is not one trick within it.

FOUR

What People Are

C. S. LEWIS WROTE to a woman in 1940 about psychoanalysis and said:

> . . . This doesn't mean that it would be wrong to try to cure a complex any more than a stiff leg; but it does mean that if you can't, then so far from the game being up, life with a complex or a stiff leg, is precisely the game you have been set. . . . We must play the parts we find ourselves given. . . . Once make the medical norm our ideal of the "normal" and we shall never lack an excuse for throwing up the sponge . . .[1]

It is tempting to draw up remarks like that and make them into something that might pass for Lewis's account of the nature of man. But that, too, would be contrary to the spirit of everything he wrote, and furthermore it would be one more manifestation of a deplorable feature of scholars who malform the materials left by another writer. It would suppose that the primary author could not have done up the nature-of-man theme had he so chosen. For Lewis, who thought long about human beings,

1. *Letters,* p. 180.

68

almost the way Samuel Johnson did, the idea becomes ridiculous. Not only did he have the skills so that he could have done what scholars do, but he would have done it with alacrity had it been admissible. Once more we are up against something rather formidable and logically guarded that keeps Lewis from an account like that. For him, that kind of descriptive account is not the way to make sense. Once more the nature of man is "shown" and it is not "said." Just why, we will once more try to ascertain by thinking anew about the morphology of Lewis's thought.

Of course, we speak in a variety of ways about the "nature" of anything. In respect to *Homo sapiens,* we often mean by "nature" that particular combination of qualities, components, and ingredients that belong to a person by birth or physical and social constitution. A theory of human nature would sketch the given and native characteristics within which growth and maturation take place. So when it is said that one cannot do much with a given individual, it is also thought that his or her "nature" is like a given reality, which puts limitations upon any artifices or art practiced upon the same. "Nature" is here contrasted with the "artificial," almost as reality is with the effects of art. Another use of the word "nature" marks out a kind, sort, or character, as when we describe a person of good nature or another book of the same nature as the last.[2]

One cannot imagine Lewis somehow denying the use of the term in the second manner just noted. But the first does give him pause. He is not willing to countenance the thoroughly modern idea that after centuries of bumbling, we are finally coming to the great breakthrough, a true and verifiable account of the nature of humankind. He sees no great need for such an account; in fact, everything in his literature seems to mitigate against it, and not because Lewis is preferring ignorance to

2. One can see these and more issues discussed in Lewis, "Nature," *Studies in Words* 2nd ed. (Cambridge: Cambridge University Press, 1967), pp. 24–74.

knowledge. Rather, he thinks that such an accounting is neither sensible, granting what human beings are, nor useful. It is the root need for such a theory that he finds so dubious, for it surely must arise from a wish to control people rather than to know them. The politics and motives are dubious and engender the confusion in logic.

But the misgivings about the depiction of the nature of humankind arise from another kind of consideration altogether. Maybe most things, even animals, can be best known by isolating their components and ingredients. Their careers are, in all probability, a permutation within the limits suggested by the parts already described. For this reason, we are concerned about the pedigree of the dog, less so about that of most people. There is a strong sense in which to know a substance is to know the elements that make it. Lewis finds it a gross naturalistic prejudice to think that the quest for the nature of humankind is going to be useful just because it was so in respect to animals. This transition cannot be made without loss. As a general tactic, the scrutinizing intellect that seeks only the same thing in respect to people as we have for everything else is nowhere so intellectually generous and uninhibited by prejudices as it may at first appear. Certainly we tend to think that only false conceptions of human dignity and a reluctance to see ourselves diagnosed must be the cause for our dismay; again Lewis thinks us wrong. In a lot of the plainperson's stubbornness to yield too quickly, or to yield at all, there is also a wide streak of sanity. There is a strong temptation among intellectuals to think that a refined kind of affection may be nothing more than a sublimated form of lust, or that justice done to the criminal may be only sublimated revenge, or that Christians and their mystical union with God in the Communion may be nothing but eating and drinking once more. Nonetheless, these too are resisted by all those who think that "nothing but" is a dubious philosophy. And the wisdom of those who resist this plausible kind of reductionism may be profound. Lewis certainly felt so.

Most general theories subsume too much, and he is entirely on the side of considering each issue separately.

As we have noted already, it is intellectually tempting to believe that if we want the true account of sexuality we must go to a psychologist who describes the lovers in a general law. The explanations by the lovers are distrusted before we have even heard them. The chivalrous medieval knight's poem cannot be taken seriously if we are trying to understand him; one repairs to a sociologist's account of the life of the Middle Ages. Lewis is skeptical of our regard for this kind of "knowledge about" or *savoir*. His notion is that another kind of knowledge is available—a *connaître;* and the latter is as different from the former as looking "along" things has been from looking "at" them. Those who look "at" have had it all their way; those who look "along" have been browbeaten.[3] So the person who talks about pain as a neural event would be misdescribing if all he or she knew was that description. Pain is something we suffer, and not to have suffered it would mean the definition would be misleading and one would not really know what one was talking about. The concept "pain" requires the suffering. Normality, honor, love, religion are even more difficult. Pain is something no one can escape; hence, we already share the knowledge that comes by suffering it. The others may be there in other people, not ourselves, but they all may be wrongly described because one does not know what they are. One has no *connaître;* and without that, they do not exist. For to have them, logically as well as psychologically, requires that they, too, be suffered.

This distinction needs to be drawn in another way to make it clearer. Lewis has also happened upon the distinction between two kinds of language that is exceedingly illuminating and helpful. His "looking along" and "looking at" metaphors do not do that distinction the justice it deserves. Would it not be better to say that there is, for example, a language "of" love

3. C. S. Lewis, "Meditation in a Toolshed," in *God in the Dock,* pp. 212–15.

that is different from the language "about" it? To learn the former requires that new kind of consciousness that Lewis has noted, the kind that a great love poet might create in us. It requires, too, that one have a passion, a feeling and an enthusiasm, with which then the language itself blends. It is not that the language of love simply expresses something nonlinguistic, albeit there is that possibility; it is that then language itself becomes a part of the loving. The language becomes one more means of loving. So, too, with morality. The language of morals is not typically "about" morals, but it becomes a means of being moral. Lewis would also have us remember that this is true of the languages of honor, faith, and patriotism.[4] To know how much is required in using each of these expressions is a good part of understanding what it means to be human. Contrariwise, to want to reduce each of these respective uses to a "core meaning" is understandable enough, but the enterprise becomes ludicrous upon detailed consideration.

Lewis's notion about human nature and giving an account of it seems to inhere in a similar reductionism. The concept "human" is such that it conflicts with the concept "nature," as ordinarily conceived. There is nothing singular to go with human. To describe people under a general accounting of their "nature" will always leave out the distinctively "human." And there is no one-to-one correspondence between these two. Love is not lust, nor is an emotion only a sensation. The concept "human" has a moral quality already. It suggests and, even more properly, actually requires that one be prepared to consider that anything given and natural be transformed and transposed into a higher key. Thus the same heart palpitations, the same rising blood pressure have to become, in turn, "fear," "surprise," and "disdain."[5] To go the other way, by analyzing

4. I draw rather heavily here upon earlier essays of mine where this has been argued. This kind of issue makes sense only if you can see it exemplified. And that exemplification takes place in Kierkegaard's writings, in Wittgenstein's *Philosophical Investigations,* along with Lewis's own works.

5. Note the sermonic essay called "Transposition," in C. S. Lewis, *The Weight of*

these emotions and finding the same sensory perturbation is only to identify mistakenly each of them. There is a radical discontinuity between them, despite their common physiology. What makes the differentia is everything like education, culture, social concern, and taste, in short, what helps us make a bit of nature into something human. There is a transposition upward that human beings bring to just about everything that makes their nature an almost useless datum. And that transposition is no single act; it goes on for a lifetime and defies description except when it is done. It is what makes every person's growth a part of one's individuality, often, in fact, the very means by which one's individuality is consummated.

The language "about" indeed is singular, and about people it is drab and uninteresting. All it can tell us is about the common factor, be it physiology, sensation, or bloodstream. The languages "of" love, faith, passion, and poetry require that the common core be caught up into all kinds of living syntheses. Not only that, they require "fear" and not just physiology, "repentance" and not just a sensation, and so on through a long list of typically human achievements. One spends a lifetime learning to be a faithful and true lover, a deeply just and dedicated champion of equity, and a stalwart advocate of one's country. Lewis's point is, I believe, a matter of recognition, not so much a proposal. It grows up in one like a dawning awareness, once one has seen what being human requires. One may start with a nature, but one ends with a truly human life.

II

Several aspects of this logic of mankind will be attempted, once more in order to do justice to Lewis's very different kind

---

Glory (Grand Rapids, Mich.: Eerdmans, 1965), paperback, pp. 16–30. But this theme was also developed in lengthy correspondence with Owen Barfield, cf. an example, *Letters,* pp. 189–91; also note the criticism of Teilhard de Chardin in the letter to Fr. Milward, pp. 295–96.

of authorship. Here despite his strong avowal of Christian orthodoxy and his ready endorsement of doctrines about humanity, God, and the world, he did not consider them to be answers by revelation to questions otherwise responded to elsewhere. Once again, their logic and force have to be separately addressed, and will be in Chapter 5. Here let us say again that human beings cannot be summarized, not because they are so various but because they do not have an essence open to the ordinary naturelike accounting.

We have just noted Lewis's concept of "transposition," which says that admittedly everything in our thought-life, our esthetic appreciation, our moral and spiritual life recurs rather plainly in our natural and physical elements. It is tempting to say that everything occurring in the former is nothing but what one has in the latter. Lewis thinks that that is a practice of judging everything from below and really also a disgraceful feature of contemporary modern thought. He is out to get it, from his earliest pages to the last. The mode of attack is, again, not direct. A direct onslaught would require the use of an "about" language to substitute for all the many languages "of" this or that.

One of the neglected features of Lewis's thought here is the extraordinarily high conception he has of human consciousness itself. That consciousness supplies the modes of the transposition. And it becomes important to remember that human beings are always conscious, while simultaneously remembering that consciousness is not something that itself can be studied directly. It can be understood, anticipated, and qualitatively appreciated; but it is not itself a "thing" or a "substance." Therefore, it becomes a very instructive remark to be told that one should ever and always treat people as conscious beings. This is, again, something like a major word, even a grammatical remark. It is to comment in such a way that a range of expectations are now in order, a mode of responses are proper, and it rules out all kinds of behavior as inappropriate.

People, to generalize a little, do not strictly speaking have a consciousness as they would a part of their nature. They "have it" in one sense, but they never have it statically. Because it is not a thing at all. It is a way of apprehending, thinking, laughing, and being variously ordered to the world and oneself. One does that to and with oneself. On the other hand, the animal is so ordered, and, therefore, its wagging tail is not a language to itself, but it may be a means of communication to its owner. The animal just wags under certain conditions. People, in contrast, are variously conscious, aware, and attentive. Their active role in this never diminishes. It is not as if one becomes conscious once-for-all and then stays that way. To say that one is conscious is not to say very much, except that one is still paying attention, looking at this or that, and generally responsive. I find Lewis's pages a remarkable collection of reminders upon what human life is all about, not because he continually sums it up, but because he collects the raw material and orders it so cogently. Not least on this issue of consciousness. He has supplied us the reminders that make the accounts of our general human nature fall away. Something more noble and correct takes its place. He gives us no general theory, but a morphologized and sense-endued human scene.

For the considerations about people being conscious do not require a doctrine about humankind being conscious. Instead one learns, therefore, an altogether different attitude. We treat and perceive people differently from things. We hold people responsible for their carelessness; but we do not morally condemn the dog who knocks over the new table. Instead we exclude it from that room. We do morals with other persons, but we do not morally condemn, no matter how much we regret, the mountain whose volcano erupts. And this confounding richness of persons means that they share my consciousness and I theirs. People cannot be objects to one another thereafter. For the consciousness we can and do share puts the humans in a different category. We are always being taught and teaching, being affected and affecting others.[6] Thus, when I read Dickens's novels, I am not only learning about nineteenth-century England. I am also, initially, sharing his consciousness. This means nothing very esoteric. It is only that I now attend to the things he attended to, feel his dismay, and exacerbate myself with an indignation over the ways things were. Of course, I do this after a while by myself. The more quickly I am exercised myself in this fashion, the more thoroughly am I taught. I may begin thinking about England, then about Dickens. Eventually, I omit both and think, feel, and talk for myself in a new way.

We have already remarked upon the significance of literature as Lewis sees it. Let us here note what this portends upon human subjects. We are never merely acted upon, as if there were only stimuli, on the one side, and responses, on the other. We are not the products of conditioning, and we are not fitted to be conditioners and trainers either. For consciousness always has to be the intervening variable, and this is not to remark upon an absurdity that creeps in and disturbs the calculus. What is absurd is the calculus! Human life, admitting the consciousness, becomes a romance and a story. This is why the epics, the allegories, and the novels have a logical correctness about them. They limn the zigzags, the mulling over, the self-corrections, the regrets and new starts better than any linear account could do. People may mature, but only their bodies develop. They have to have a literature, precisely because without it they cannot be understood. Literature shows the form of a human life without reducing it to a feature of nature.

More than that, the forms of consciousness are achieved only by the self-engendered activities. We become conscious by thinking in a certain way, by laughing at certain things and not others, by attending to this rather than that. Our lives become rich and variegated by our successes in these respects. We have to be alive to be conscious. The tingling and exciting character

6. Again note Lewis's first essay in *The Personal Heresy*.

of Lewis's writings seems to me to inhere in this almost boyish manner he has of taking the reader in hand and showing him one thing after another. All of that is not only a pleasing personal attribute; it is also a requisite of his understanding of human nature. Now we can begin to see, herewith, why the stake is high for every person. That consciousness is not a datum at all. We are not born with it, only with the possibility of it. And a moral consciousness turns out not to be so much a special mode or kind of training as much as it does the maximizing of our attention on two things—the way the world is and the way the subject, himself or herself, actually is. Getting those two straight is more than half the battle. It is almost all of it. Once one has those two, no matter how much other information is around, then what we call a moral consciousness is already present.[7] Morality is not a fever or a heightened and artificial kind of consciousness at all.

III

Another factor looms up in Lewis's writing about our common human nature. This has to do with our radical individuality, an individuality that again is not simply numerical and physical. It would be one thing to know that each person is different, so that every set of people would be made up of entities, no two quite the same. It is something else to give an account of that individuality and to see it not only as a datum but also as an achievement to be cherished and made richer and more substantial as one's life goes by. Surely the individuality is natural and a datum; but the personality is not. The latter is his view, and one begins to see it as a life unrolls, as a kind of self-management begins to develop and as, finally, a self-ownership has also to be achieved and then given up in Christian

7. Note Lewis's discussion under "The Fall," in *A Preface to Paradise Lost,* pp. 121ff.

obedience. However, until there is an individual self there to be understood, cherished, and loved, it can hardly be sacrified and denied; so the process of becoming a self and a personality and being conscious of that self are necessary and constitutive.

Once more this kind of outlook on human beings cannot be easily summarized. In a bold sense, it cannot be said; instead it has to be exemplified, and this is what Lewis's literature finally does. The reasons are several. Human beings are not contained in the protoplasm the way an oak is in the acorn. If they were, then Alexander Pope's maxim would obtain:

> The first Almighty Cause
> Acts not by partial,
> but by general laws.[8]

All kinds of other things keep entering in. Because human beings are truly individuals and potentially personalities, there is a sense in which no general law explains all of them. Lewis will not, therefore, resign all notions of rationality, order, and rule in respect to them either. Radical individuality does not imply inexplicability or simply random behavior, or mean that nothing is intelligible about them. The more subtle factor is that the intelligibility has to be achieved from within. An example might be in order. Mark Studdock is the young social scientist, newly married, rather ambitious, a member of a college faculty, but now sorely tempted to join forces with N.I.C.E., a new and enterprising fusion between state and science upon "which so many thoughtful people base their hopes of a better world." Furthermore, with the prospect of putting political power behind a deterministic and predictive science, Mark can also revel in the notion that the day of free-lance science is over, that we can create a new humanity, that "man has got to take charge of man" in order to produce a "new type of man."[9] Amid all

8. Quoted by Lewis and discussed and amplified in *Letters to Malcolm* (New York: Harcourt, Brace and World, 1964), pp. 51–56.

9. All of this is the major subject matter of *That Hideous Strength* and the quotations are from pp. 22 and 46, respectively.

that heady confusion, Mark suddenly no longer understands himself, his wife, and his modest role in his college and discipline. Everything certain begins to fade from him just as he is entering the most enthralling and comprehensive scheme he has yet encountered.

This irony of being a person Lewis clearly depicts. Just because we are actually individuals, these highly generalized schemes do not work for us. We are not herring in the shoal whose individual teleology can be read off that of the group. The more Mark becomes identified with the Belbury group the less identity he himself has and knows. Lewis would have us all remember that the more we identify with the modern age and the spirit of the times, the less likely we are to be clear about ourselves. The threat of even the inner circle we are always trying to get into, where the power is and things are happening, is that when we get in, where everything supposedly matters, we find that our lives grow so blurred and shapeless that we have lost more than we gained.

There is a fine polemical edge on most of what Lewis writes. Not unlike many moralists and Christian writers, he has to articulate his reflections against the ethos of the day. There is nothing democratic about morals and faith, if we expect that all decision of what is of worth and what can be believed is going to be decided by majority rule. Nothing that we have said here about common sense and the shape of human life ought to implicate Lewis in notions that majority rule has to prevail in morals, esthetics, science, or matters of faith. On the contrary, in all of these areas the crowd and its mentality has to be kept at bay. The only access to any of these arenas is by individuals fighting their way to conclusiveness and insight. Going along with the age is sure doom. So, too, of course, is the notion that "I am special" and no one else is. This kind of self-conception is the danger of individualism and can easily lead to the false idea that one's difference bestows a privilege.[10]

10. Note the letter to an unnamed woman, June 20, 1952, in *Letters,* pp. 242–43.

The task is to know that there is indeed a crowd and collectivities, but that we are never dignified by being like everyone else; likewise, to know that no one is like anyone else is not to separate ourselves from others, for we are fellow members, necessary to all and to each other. The individualism Lewis discloses has a deeper core. The young social scientist, Mark Studdock, one day, amid his confusion and lack of self-assurance, meets the fusty and somewhat antiquated but benign lover of literature and language, Professor Dimble. The latter is amiable and a long-time good friend of Mark's wife. Seeking help, Mark is told rather brusquely by Dimble: "I do not 'know' you. . . . I have no conception of your aims or motives."[11] This remark cuts deep, for Mark does not have an aim for himself any longer, and whatever motivation there is lacks clarity. Without aim and motive, there is literally nothing to know. He is no longer really a person; he is a tool for others. Right here, we get a picture of what being a self involves for Lewis. For there can be no self, no person, until there are aims, wishes, hopes, and pleasures. And these do not come until we begin to want, wish, care, and decide something. All of these require initiative and origination within the person. By these and these alone true selfhood is achieved.

This is why being a person is not a mechanical or purely physical matter. One becomes a person by activities and capacities that are, in turn, individually rooted. Mark does not become a person, again, until he gives up his complicity in the shadowy Institute and begins to resist all the conformity. Even ideas come with effort, and they turn out to be hard to maintain and to think, for individual effort is needed. Policies, on the other hand, go on objectively and impersonally and one hardly needs to acknowledge them. More strongly, though, we can say that all of this is directed by Lewis at two extremes that seem to be altogether too easy to come by in our day.

11. *That Hideous Strength,* p. 269.

Lewis is cognizant that collectivisms can easily make us think that "church," "state," and "science" are more important than a person, and this kind of error he combats in a variety of ways.[12] The other extreme is to pick up the idea of numerical identity and try to glorify the individual as though he were intrinsically and naturally precious. Then we get personality theory, which suggests that this treasure within must be expanded and expressed, cultivated and, above all, never suppressed. The first produces the romanticism of big government, the wedding of hope with learning, and finally a suppression of true individuality in presumably more ethical causes. Here ethicality means the loss of personality. The other outlook requires originality, and it makes ethical disciplining, culture, inherited values, and tradition look like encumbrances upon freedom, novelty, and human genuineness. Once more, there is a kind of dichotomy presented, which makes the achievement of personality look as though it could be independent of literature, morals, faith, and even personal consideration and care.

Lewis's contrast with all of this is marked. He is flatly denying the inestimable worth of human life, at least if this is supposed to mean that each instance has a natural claim upon it. He is denying, too, that each life gets worth only by identifying with social entities, or with the *Geist* of all of history. Instead he is making the immodest and striking assertion that each human life is glorious and so full of potential because personality is not a datum at all. It is an achievement, and Christians will have it that its realization is very far ahead. Instead of the key to this development lying simply within ourselves, as if it will all unfold, Lewis finds that our will is indeed involved. But we have to choose and to occupy those places for which we are fitted. Even becoming moral is not a matter of inventing a value,

12. Note his essay, "Membership," which appears in *The Weight of Glory*, pp. 30–43 and, also, in *Fern-Seed and Elephants*, ed. Walter Hooper (London: Fontana/Collins, 1975), pp. 11–26.

then realizing it. It is like the moral order and reality being there already, and the changes have to be made in us. The drama of becoming a personality is not to assert oneself against everybody and everything as much as it lies in becoming self-cognizant and learning to do what one must. Once more, indirection is the clue. If we find the truth and then tell it, do the work for its own sake, love with all our hearts, it is Lewis's confidence that the personality and character will come forth, original and lovely to know and to be.

The clarification does not come by espousing theories of personality any more than it does by praising general sketches of the good life. Here the issues are not just matters of hypocrisies and saying more than one's life will bear out; but again the matter has to do with the very logic of personality. It is this which gives Lewis's literature such formidable quality. That logic of moral achievement by which an individual is turned into a personality is like a firm structure tying all the parts of his writings together. This is why there is something philosophical and a little grave about his authorship and that keeps it from becoming only a pastiche or a glittering outcropping of his genius.

I speak here of the logic of personality, not of a theory of personality. As we read we get a picture something like this. If we think of those who have never "cared for" great music, never had a friend, never been a lover, never enjoyed a good joke, seldom relished a meal, never felt the tang of cold air with zestiness, then we are beginning to understand why we find some people to be almost without personality. We do not ask that they be for athletics or value culture. That is much too abstract. But to have relished, laughed, cried, enjoyed a host of specific things is what adds up after a while. Then we can transpose upward and think about the person for whom the difference between good and evil is not momentous, whose conscience is inoperative, who does not care whether cruelty toward others obtains, and who sees little in whether he is right or wrong, then we surely begin to see, once more, that a personality is at stake. In the latter case, where there is no moral pathos, we have the nadir of personality and the death of self. This is the state of damnation.

Lewis's literature is one long essay in showing us how these little things do finally make up our lives. In bold it might be said that it is not moral theories that save their proponents but, it is how quickly and thoroughly the small tasks are taken up. The characters in the Narnia *Chronicles* are broken and made, depending upon how well they do that. And most of those animals are like hieroglyphs for human beings. The logic of their lives stands out after a bit. One sees that the qualities of human subjectivity, the anxieties, the frustrations, the torments are like the field of obstacles and exercises, which to conquer is to gain in stature and to grow in spirit. There is no other way.

IV

Lewis's reflections are everywhere characterized by great balance and a careful consideration of the relevant details. He refuses to conclude that orthodox Christian teachings do not allow for genuine esthetic and ethical achievements, this despite the severity of the doctrine of sin. By the same token, he does not disallow the achievements of Greek and Roman culture, this despite the later and superb benefits of Christ and the salvation he proffers. We read Lewis's pages sometimes just to learn how to savor the sagas, the doomed Eddaic gods, the *Roman de la Rose,* strange myths, and stranger long poems. Besides, Lewis includes the entire Christian story. The striking feature of all of this is that everything seems somehow to count. People seem to be like that to him.

Unlike most contemporary thinkers, Lewis proposes a radically different perspective for all to share. Most of us have been taught to feel ourselves confronted with a reality, both natural and historical, whose import we can never actually know. The skeptics insist that there is no significance in it and that the quest is pointless. The antimetaphysical notions run very deep. Braver souls want to say that poets, or at least those with a refined sensibility, can either invent a meaning out of their peculiar subjectivity or attribute a shape, where reality had neither. Then human beings must vacillate, on the one side, between a positivism that finds all the laws and order in the sciences to be mind-contributed, and, on the other side, a cult that makes literary geniuses the new guarantors of meaning and humaneness. The logic of that kind of skepticism calls up the very peculiar picture of Promethean man, who has to stem the tide of meaninglessness and defy reality itself. There is something quite different about Lewis's demeanor and style here. He is not one to think that a puny creature called man has to awaken nature into order, life, and beauty. The story of literature alone will not bear that out.[13] If one takes the very long look, as Lewis did over a lifetime, reality takes care of itself. It needs no interpretation and no intellectual gloss in order to acquire its force and relevance. The adaptations have to be made in the subjects, the people, who have to learn what is already there. The perfection, beauty, goodness, and worth are already part of reality—what is lacking is something in the subject for whom it has still to be an achievement of insight, imagination, and taste.

All of this says something about what human subjects are. When someone adapts even to the array of literature, that person need not glean from it only evidence for an argument; instead it is as if that wonderful totality leaves a print, a form, in the reader by which understanding is ordered. Lewis tells us in his book *The Discarded Image* that Isadore makes even

13. J. A. W. Bennett, "Grete Clerk," in *Light on C. S. Lewis,* ed. Jocelyn Gibb (New York, 1965), pp. 44–51. Also note Bennett's essay, *The Humane Medievalist* (Cambridge: Cambridge University Press, 1965) for another assessment of Lewis, relevant to this consideration.

history a department of grammar. Here is an extended use of the concept of grammar, far beyond the modest realm it describes today. Lewis conjectures that Isadore would have described *The Discarded Image* as a book of "Grammar."[14] And, in a way, that is also to say that persons are grammar-prone. It is not only to a sophisticated and highly self-conscious frame of mind that the literature and reality begins to address itself. Once more, "receptivity," not just an informed inquisitiveness, is what is requisite. And people can receive that print of reality itself.

We need to recover something of a child's lust for the marvels and the exciting fear of hobgoblins, of the young person's zest for hazards and danger, of the young adult's cry for physical beauty and truth. Lewis's point is that our common human nature includes these capacities and that only by them will we really be at home in the objective world. Reality itself is not made by our interests, but it is known by them. This means that human beings are not merely slivers of will that must live by decisions—that excess of modern existentialism is again produced only by forgetfulness of what we have just noted. We become personalities only by having a heart, by developing a warmth and compassion, and living in love and hope. None of these is decorative. Neither are we logical machines and "pure" thinkers. The idealization of people around the notion of their being only rational is another extravagance. People need to feel correctly about something in order to know properly what reality is. Both romanticism and classicism can make their point, but neither is true by itself. Our obligation is to the way things are, and things need and entail the pleasures, the responses, the feelings, and the thoughts. To miss all that by partial views and half-developed lives is to condemn not reality but our own character. Character formation is what is at stake.

14. *The Discarded Image: An Introduction to Medieval and Renaissance Literature* (Cambridge: Cambridge University Press, 1964), p. 187.

Once more we begin to see what human beings actually are and how important the quality of a life turns out to be.

And there is more. As we have already noted, Lewis is very clear that human personality is not the radiant goal for all ethical striving. He finds that the modern cult to the effect that personality is ultimately precious, that everyone is original, that creativity is what matters most—all of that is plainly rubbish. These views are not just wrong, they are without meaning; for they have nothing whatsoever to fit. There is no notion that the development of the personality is the sole ethical goal of our common life or that it is the principal value. Saying all that, we now must say something more about subjectivity and the self. Few authors have such a regard for the qualities of subjectivity, while simultaneously insisting that that subjectivity is not the chief value and decrying a romanticism that denigrates objectivity. Lewis puts together the plea for objectivity with a portrayal of the richness of human subjectivity.

The point is, I believe, that Lewis has seen in all of this that the self is both a recipient of a host of things and also an active agent. More properly, the self is a relation, not a thing. The personality is neither godlike and truly original, nor simply an effect and made only by externals. It is both made and maker, debtor and giver. This again requires another kind of schematism by which it can be thought and entertained. I choose here to exploit an example from a book that is not one of Lewis's most popular.[15] I could have used any number of examples that are analogically explored in his works. The effect of these examples makes another kind of notion take shape in our minds. It is as if the essence of becoming a person becomes clear to us as the psychological facts and procedures get established. Here, however, I refer only to one instance.

The issue is why "praising" is demanded of people by God. There is a sense in which this seems like a miserable idea, as if

15. *Reflections on the Psalms* (London: Geoffrey Bles, 1958). Cf. esp. chap. IX.

God craves praise the way a vain person wants compliments, or the way an anxious author pleads for recognition, or the way a dog needs the continual gratification of attention. Lewis knew the familiar uses of praise to be complimenting, approving, and giving of just honor. Granted that God is magisterial and worthy, then the praise is both appropriate and yet, oddly enough, a little strange to read in the psalms as continually commanded. What sense, then, does the idea of praising, and continually so, make?

Another kind of practical logic is brought to our attention. Thinking almost like Aristotle, Lewis turns to a host of relations between subjective factors. And the fact that there are these relations that hold in the subjective arena begins to tell you what a subject actually is. The logic of the relations tells you what that self is. Two contrasting cases are cited. We get a picture drawn of how enjoyment, zestful fun, and pleasure spontaneously overflow into praise. Thus, a lover praises the beloved, hikers the spring weather, the wine drinker the new crop, a happy college student the "alma mater," the golfer a par game, the student a favorite professor, the healthy person the bracing air. The point is that often enjoyment and praise are spontaneously related. Lewis does not suggest that an intellectual model is necessary, namely, that a judgment is formed that says X is praiseworthy. Both enjoying something and praising are like unmediated responses. Once more we have to be able to enjoy the good food; and when we do, we say: "Great! Excellent! Wasn't that a good one?" The praise flows like the enjoyment.

Lewis's point is that the quality of the minds (and of the persons) is exceedingly important to remark upon. The other extreme is the person for whom no animal is of any interest, no meal up to standard, no book worth anything but a critical remark, no historical personage anything but odd. One would be wrong at this juncture to conclude that those differences are merely a matter of opinion or degree of evidence. Equally, one would be mistaken in thinking that the objective facts are all that matter. Lewis, with all his regard for objectivity and for the objectivity of moral and natural law, will never allow himself to lapse into this typical twentieth-century view. His regard for human subjectivity and the role of personality is far too great.

This is not a case of one person seeing different facts and praising, the other individual looking at something else and grumbling. The burden may lie with "which" facts; but Lewis is concerned with "seeing." One person perceives what is there, while the other person does not. Readers of the Narnia stories will recognize all kinds of instances immediately. "Seeing" is not automatic, neither is hearing or feeling or thinking. The subject behind the activity will limit or extend the possibilities, depending upon what and who he or she is.

We then get another kind of logic altogether thrown into the scene. About "praise" again, Lewis says simply that ". . . the humblest, and at the same time, most balanced and capacious, minds, praised most, while the cranks, misfits and malcontents praised least." Dyspeptic and snobbish critics find little to praise; anxious lovers can't enjoy each other; frightened thinkers can't savor any idea except those already approved. Now the whole picture begins to change. The healthy person, not victimized by popular fads, will, even if brought up in luxury, find a delight in a modest meal, where the cad will revel in it if "simplicity" is a reigning idea or despise it if "epicure" notions prevail.

The logic of the self is what is so interesting in all of this. One picture, a crudely intellectualized one, is misleading and falsifying. It would picture the self as a *tabula rasa,* receiving the "sensations," synthesizing them, focusing ideas, testing them in relation to things, and issuing finally in judgments. Praise or no praise would depend upon a prior ratiocination. So, too, with God. Then the objectivities would be met by a judging intellect, who then would so formulate an account of what is the case, that subjectivity would follow as a matter of course. However, this entire scenario is rewritten in the Lewis literature. The separation of emotions, judgments, feelings, and thoughts is not directly addressed, but that separation is rendered hapless by the kind of example we have noted.

In that context, where enjoying one's love issues in praise of the beloved, the depiction of "enjoy" and "praise" as verbs, is that they, too, are ways to relate to the objective world. They are verbs with objects. One does not, while "enjoying," also secretly and inwardly "know," simultaneously and silently. No, the enjoying, the loving, the eating, the smelling—all these and more are part of the synthesis that the self, the person, continually makes with objective things. The account of the self is that its capaciousness, its roominess, its capabilities determine the account that is given of the world. And it is not by abstracting from love, care, feeling—and finding a bare transcendental ego, the "pure" thought—that one will get intellectual agreement at all. That representation is wrong. We do not get true objectivity and consensus by stripping off pathos, passion, and enjoyment, and sharing some bare minimum; instead, we get consensus and even praise together, when we share the other factors that form deeply true human lives.

This is why Lewis's literature is so profound and so different. It is as if he has happened upon fundamental matters in simply doing the best small tasks of which he was capable. The big issues loom up after a while, almost graphically projecting a conception that no one seems to have written. Selfhood manifests itself in an objective way too. The self is a nest of capabilities, formed and made, so that its knowing is part of the enjoying, loving, and praising. The agreement between people depends, indeed, upon there being an objective world. The question is, How do we come to know it? That agreement on what is what is itself dependent upon our having a life so formed as to be capable of knowing it. "Knowing" is an abstract expression; mostly we know when we enjoy, love, praise, and care for the things around us. This is what goes into being a knower.

We are not then *tabula rasa* at all. We are active knowers, not passive. What we know depends upon the kind of person we have made of ourselves. The world's infinite riches, its values and worths, its pleasures and depths can be found only if we are qualified subjects. Put affirmatively this means that each of us has a richness of personal life for which we are uniquely responsible. We have a treasure to guard in ourselves that is our richness.

FIVE

On Theology and God

IT IS A COMMONPLACE among us that we live amid the decay of our moral and cultural traditions. Since World War I it has been almost routine to say that massive social problems are somehow the responsibility of the churches. Thus our cities have a massive crime problem and then, in turn, the ministers along with others call for a more rigorous enforcement of the law by the police and the judges. In the same context it is easy to concur with a leading theologian who said that all of this is "a nice admission of defeat upon the part of the church."[1] That, finally, is the way that many people in the past few decades have viewed Christianity, the church, and the ministers, namely, as if they must both articulate the old moral and cultural traditions, on the one hand, and then, second, so modify those traditions that each individual, in whatever new circumstances, will save his or her life and also that of society, from moral anarchy.

1. This was said by Reinhold Niebuhr, in *Leaves from the Notebook of a Tamed Cynic* (New York: Willett, Clark and Colby, 1929) p. 116. The same kind of remark could be cited by those who tell us about "the loss of credibility of the modern church," of the irrelevance of the ministry, and of the need for a new theology pertinent to urban life, to science, and to an industrial society.

C. S. Lewis lived through a period in English life when the intellectuals and the esthetes were anti-Christian and certainly highly critical of the role of the church. But the temper of that disparagement was not like that of the American scene. England never suffered the indignity of H. L. Mencken and the Scopes trial. The extremes were muted. Besides, the evangelical Christian movements in England were and are of very long standing, and they never quite produced the popular forms of fundamentalism and anti-intellectualism that America spawned. The battle lines were not so dramatically drawn between liberals and conservatives, orthodox and modernists. Instead there was an accelerated erosion of that gentle kind of English social and political humanism that assimilated Christianity into an ordered society, a society characterized by mutual interdependence and public service. English religious life was more Erasmian, almost as if the nature of the best commonwealth could be created by the social function of the *philosophia Christi.* [2] The Christian teaching had been long an ingredient in English social and cultural life in a rich variety of ways. The church and its ministers seemed to service that common life in a host of styles and purposes.

Lewis is not one to lament the passing of this kind of religiosity. He agrees it has passed away and that we are living in a post-Christian era, but he puts this in a very guarded way. The decline of religion is ambiguous to him and not without its clarifying side too. What had happened during earlier periods was something like the creation of a social order, a kind of Christendom, where a vague spirituality and theism ". . . with a strong and virile ethical code, which, far from standing over against the 'World,' was absorbed into the whole fabric of

2. The reference here is to Erasmus, the gentle contemporary of Luther and Calvin, who edited Plato's works and also the Latin and the Greek texts of the New Testament. His *Paraphrases* on the latter became, after 1548, almost a standard for the reading and preaching of the gospel in the Church of England.

English institutions and sentiment and therefore demanded church-going as (at best) a part of loyalty and good manners as (at most) a proof of respectability."[3] But all of that was not Christianity—it was "morality tinged with emotion," "what a man does with his solitude," and "a generalized religion using Christian terms."

Lewis could scarcely disregard the obvious fact that the intellectuals also had been disregarding Christianity for a long time. Shelley, William Morris, Thackeray, Meredith, Swinburne, Hardy, Trollope, and numerous scientists and philosophers of the past century and a half have written books that are neither by nor for people who think of the likelihood of damnation, the possibility of miracles, the incarnation of God in Jesus Christ, or the magnitude of sin. Certainly the main currents of American arts, science, and letters describe a similar course. The other fact is plain enough, there is an unchristening in the public domain. The notion that the skepticism and antifaith talk is all due to increasing maturation, new discoveries, better understanding, and a general improvement in the race—all of that Lewis finds to be false.

Lewis's apologetic literature has a different slant from what one might imagine. For one thing, it articulates Christianity in terms that are for many unfamiliar, mostly because they do not grow out of the obvious religious and social terrain. He has little interest in resuscitating that kind of mild social theism once more. Here he reminds one a bit of Søren Kierkegaard (1813–55), the Danish man of letters, who also thought that a major task now was to reintroduce Christianity into Christendom, where everyone already assumed they knew what it was. And whatever one can make of Dietrich Bonhoeffer's incomplete reflections, it also seems that he, too, was concluding that the social amalgam that made up the German Christian outlook

---

3. C. S. Lewis, "The Decline of Religion," in *God in the Dock*, pp. 219–20. Note also his "De Descriptione Temporum," in *Selected Literary Essays*, pp. 4–6.

and practice between the wars needed to be winnowed and gleaned before one could find the rudiments of genuine Christianity. Lewis, however, does his task in the vernacular. By that I mean that he does not choose to invent a new theology or a new philosophical system by which to restate the Christian teachings. With the attempts to translate those teachings into allegories or to rephrase the Christian story as a myth or a principle, so that one will entertain their meaning in some other form, with all of that, Lewis has nothing whatever to do. If anything, Lewis moves out of the theological and out of the philosophical and into the ordinary language of everyday life. "Any fool," he notes, "can write 'learned' language. The vernacular is the real test. If you can't turn your faith into it, then either you don't understand it or you don't believe it."[4]

Though he addressed the learned community in the interest of crediting the concept of miracles and again with the problem of "pain," his focus there is not to supply an alternative to what he thinks are the false philosophies so much as to get some views out of the way that discredit in advance the ordinary ways of talking, believing, and behaving. It is as if there are plain, primary, first-order ways of thinking and speaking that have to be restored to people before they can make any sense of the Christian literature. Perhaps there is an analogue here to what we noted about the reading of great literature, namely, that one can have it spoiled by always viewing it through a literary theory and seldom if ever relishing the story and savoring the actual lines of poetry.

Already we have indicated a kind of new ordering of thoughts going on in Lewis's writing about God and theological matters. It seems clear enough that Lewis is not a success as an

---

4. "Letters," included in *God in the Dock*, p. 338. Originally these remarks were printed in the *Christian Century*, vol. LXXV (December 1958), in an exchange with W. Norman Pittenger. See also the letter to Professor Clyde S. Kilby in *Letters of C. S. Lewis*, pp. 273–74.

apologist because he was a vulgarizer or a crude popularizer. Neither is he reidentifying Christian themes so that they will somehow coalesce with interests that are already current. Nor is he proffering a panacea for the social ills, nor a restoration of human happiness, nor a relief to all the nagging anxieties of the war years.

Here I wish to sketch how his reflections about God and things Christian also have assumed quite a different shape. It seems to me that this is far tougher and far more original and acute than most of his readers have surmised. Admittedly, Lewis is eminently talented and gracefully learned and, therefore, he can make his writing vivid and his points attractive by sheer talent and an extravagance of personal forces. He is virtuosic, so that the rest of us who are usually debtors and pedants and followers by necessity, can scarcely fail to be instructed. But there is more to his religious writing than trickery and sheer brilliance of performance. There is also more than pandering to a populace and succoring the crowd.

There is a reshaping of thinking itself, of the whole mode and manner of ideation and reflection that Christianity requires. Correlative to this, however, is the discovery by him of the very language of faith and, consequently, a new understanding for Lewis of the language that Christian people naturally and spontaneously speak. This way of speaking has strong affinities with the Bible itself, but it is also more immediately appealing to human beings. It is "ordinary" and ordered to the everyday concerns of the human heart. The point that is tellingly made is that this is not "theological" in the manner of the professional theologians, any more than epic poetry or good stories are only disguised instances of literary theory. It was Lewis's confidence in that way of addressing the issues that made his pages and his public addresses so immediately arresting.

C. S. Lewis came to this recognition and competence in a new way of understanding, thinking, and speaking, not out of the tendentious give and take of epistemology, of logic, or of concept-analysis. Though he was qualified initially to tutor in phi-losophy and did so in an Oxford college, it was not by philo-sophical or theological argument that he reshaped his concep-tual grasp. It was by having his thought-life formed and accommodated to the flow of literature and what it is about, nontheoretical and in a variety of styles and moods, on the one side, and to the New Testament and what it is about, on the other. Out of all that came a recognition of rich differences and the clear and almost uncanny and fresh way Lewis has of addressing people in a moral and Christian interest.

Lewis is not justly characterized by saying that he is a con-servative rather than a modernist, or that he is orthodox, con-ventional, and a rationalist. There are circumstances within which those remarks become telling; but there is something deeper and more exciting about Lewis's thought that is seldom noticed. He has accommodated and adjusted his reflections in a series of very small moves; but these at once put him outside those rather cursory descriptive positions we have cited and free him from the structures of the ordinary position-taking and typical pedagogical schemes within which most of us are taught to think. In Lewis's case this means that he can read and think himself back into the New Testament, to a variety of myths and fairytales, to the ordinary discourse in which moral, passional, and momentous concerns are initially couched. It is as if or-thodoxy's substance can now be assimilated without the ar-tifices of scholasticism, as if the urgencies of the New Testament can be secured without the formidable intellectual contrivances of fundamentalism, as if the heights and depths of a spiritual life can be incorporated without being anti-intellectual, irre-sponsibly romantic, or theologically liberal. In this context I find Lewis's manner and mode of thought a major achievement.

Surely it is forged in part by his discovery of how there is a logic to allegory, a rule for metaphor, a set of congruences between what is said and how it is being said. It is brought about also by his rediscovery of not only how literature and teachings tell us something or other, but how they stimulate and sustain in us (even where they tell us something) new capacities and powers. The give and take with theoretical matters is there in his pages, but this does not force him always to erect one more thing himself. Instead, he has seen and has done with us (and for us), in both his fiction and writings in the "about" mood, that kind of writing that forces us to another kind of endeavor, one that cannot be done on paper or in a book. Thus, he does not say a word calculated to help anyone to decide between denominations or rival theological views, but he does seek to get us to believe in God and Jesus Christ.[5] It is too simple to say that this is only a matter of stressing the minimal teachings or the lowest common denominator. The form of one's thought has to be different even to get at that "mere" Christianity. But that is to anticipate our next pages, wherein we will now note that issue, plus the remarkable manner in which Lewis puts his literary and imaginative skills to the task of seeing Christianity from the inside.

II

In a letter to a former pupil, Lewis wrote:

> The process of living seems to consist in coming to realize truths as ancient and simple that, if stated, they sound like barren platitudes. They cannot sound otherwise to those who have not had the relevant experience: that is why there is no real teaching of such truths possible and every generation starts from scratch. . . .

To the same person, almost two decades later, he writes, "The gradual 'reading' of one's own life, seeing a pattern emerge, is a great illumination at our age."[6] Obviously two things are tied

5. Note here the new Preface to *Mere Christianity* (1952), where Lewis explains why *The Case for Christianity, Christian Behavior,* and *Beyond Personality* did not stress theological "isms" and doctrinal issues.

6. Two letters to Dom Bede Griffith, O.S.B., 1939 and 1956. In *Letters,* pp. 166, 266.

together—truths old and simple, and a reading and understanding of oneself. If we have been right in our previous chapters,
either of these sooner or later entails the other. But this leaves
still unsettled the question how they are related.

It seems to be something like this. The grand yet simple
theological truths that Lewis has such a strong concern for are
actually the elementary and plain assertions that make up the
gospel itself. These are the kerygma, the rudimentary components making up the evangel, summarized in the creed of the
apostles. Lewis did not consider these to be theology in the
modern sense, nor were these teachings to be thought of as
second-order meditations upon the primary material. This
group of very elementary sayings were truly the "what," the
elements; and they were for Lewis not, in the ordinary senses,
a point of view, an angle upon the facts, or an optional view.
Lewis dared to treat these teachings as simply the ways in
which an individual learns and says what is the case. They are
the facts.

Saying they are the facts sounds dogmatic and intolerant, and
the tendency in our time is to suggest that we never can know
the facts in themselves; instead we always have only a point of
view, a kind of theology, on the facts. It becomes as close as we
get. Here is where Lewis parts company with the popular
thought of the age. He does not only insist or declaim that these
are the facts; for establishing the facts by rhetoric would be
truly irrational and dogmatic in an invidious sense. Instead, he
draws attention to a deeper side of our rational and intellectual
life and nature. His early philosophical training and his very
acute intelligence got him to steer another course.[7] The grand
philosophical tradition he was trained in, philosophical idealism, gave what was purported to be a definitive and certain
meaning to fundamental words like "rational" and "fact"; and
it endeavored to establish a standard and necessary kind of

7. His autobiography, *Surprised by Joy,* is most appropriate here.

logic and epistemology within which all learning, of whatever one pleased, from biology to theology, from history to literary criticism, would be judged and understood and described. The notion of a general kind of "rationality," or a singular standard and defensible way of defining truth and reality, has been long-term in Western thought. Lewis witnessed in his own time a grand change in the acceptable Anglo-American patterns of reflection. The old kind of pan-logical idealism disappeared and with it a congeniality toward older values and certainly a type of theism too. It was replaced by a more scientifically oriented philosophical scheme. Broadly speaking, for Lewis it was described as a "naturalism." It invoked criteria of evidence, of science (rather crudely described perhaps), and of meaning. Eventually this kind of naturalism was stylized under the rubric of "positivism" and later found another formulation under "analytic philosophy." The attitudinal core of these movements is what he is concerned about.

Our point is that Lewis is quarreling not with individuals (Ryle, Bradley, Wittgenstein, or Russell, say, on this or that precise view) as much as he is with those kinds of thought often engendered by them and transmuted into tacit beliefs among his contemporaries. These beliefs make miracles seem impossible, they keep us from believing that any sense or meaning can obtain anywhere in myths, poems, miracles, Bible, fairy tales, and traditional morals. Lewis is not convinced of a standard "rationality," which must exclude God, miracles, heaven, hell, and a lot more. Against that tendency in Western thought to move from one extreme to another, from classicism to romanticism, from reason to emotion, from a standard to arbitrariness, from intellectualism to anti-intellectualism, Lewis proposes something else altogether. He is opposed to ideological extremes of this sort. He is an advocate of order, criteria, and norms, of logic, sense, and rules of meaning—in short, he talks about rationality against the new irrationalities and in Christian matters as elsewhere. About this there is no doubt. His discovery is that there is no single and univocal way of being rational; for rationality cannot altogether exclude emotion, it cannot say all myths are prescientific and leave matters at that, it cannot be coolly detached and exclude a life of feelings and pathos. What one excludes or includes, what one judges negatively or describes invidiously, depends upon the subject matter one is considering and the relevant capacities that are necessitated to see, to know, and to understand.[8]

Lewis knew how tempting it was in Christian circles to move with the times. Christians, too, once redefined the content of the faith to get it into the commodious idealistic and standarized rational scheme that its logic and its rules suggest. A certain kind of "theology" was written, trying to translate, usually by both elimination and a reshuffling of the issues under new concepts, the major primary teachings. Later the new kinds of positivism led to different general notions of "meaningfulness" and method, even of logic and sense. We now have God-is-dead talk and the extremes of current liberal theology, which feel it necessary to get rid of everything that is not either scientific or "meaningful" to modern man.[9]

The picture is dismal, for it means that we are invariably imprisoned in these large philosophical or quasi-theological views before we can speak about specific Christian issues. There seems to be no primary language at all. All apprehension and knowing of Christian things is via the theology or the second-level discourse. Furthermore, that keeps changing and no agreement upon it is possible. Lewis's discovery of Christianity was plainly a rather momentous event for him. But he seems not to have been converted to a theological scheme at all, and

8. One can consider here Lewis's *Pilgrim's Regress* as an apt try at picturing a kind of rationality that must include also the features of romanticism. *Till We Have Faces* is another and more acute fictional attempt. Note also "At the Fringe of Language," in C. S. Lewis, *Studies in Words,* pp. 313ff.

9. Lewis's writings on these issues are numerous. Note his "Modern Theology and Biblical Criticism" and "Historicism," in *Christian Reflections.*

he refused all of his life to think that an understanding of Christianity would necessitate that he adopt an elaborate theology.

The fact that Lewis was attracted to those simple kerygmatic teachings did, obviously enough, bring him into the main stream of orthodoxy. For Catholics and most Protestants avow in their confessional books and by their use of the Apostles' Creed that in some way or another those elementary truths are crucial. The practice of the intellectuals, however, seems always to suggest that we must have a theological view in order to use that material, or even worse, it is suggested that those teachings already represent a point of view or a second-level outlook. This is what Lewis denies. What he calls "mere" Christianity is that range of teachings indeed, and it is the common core of most churches. What it requires is not translation into a new and better conceptual system; it enjoins a refashioning of the individual. The accommodation has to be made by the individual to those facts—the changes are many and subtle. The primeval moral platitudes, the requirement to be just, courageous, and temperate, these and more now begin to make sense. They force the individual to another way of thinking, living, and even perceiving the world. No wonder moral requisites could be like schoolmasters preparing us for becoming Christians. Christianity is, as Lewis saw it, early and late, just about the last subject in which to attempt originality. It neither needed it nor could finally use it.[10]

All of this probably suggests something else to the modern reader. Anyone who dares to say that the biblical narratives and creedal statements are to be taken with seriousness is immediately accused of being a "literalist" and also a "fundamentalist." It sounds as though a theological position is truly inescapable and that "no position" becomes a blatant kind of anti-intellectualism, masquerading under a dogmatic declara-

10. Note again the Preface to *Mere Christianity*.

tion of the authority of Scripture. Lewis, because of his avowal of those central affirmations and his espousal of what the Bible says, has seemed to many a throwback, an intellectual who wants certainty at any price. His accusers think of him as a peculiar artifact, an intellectual anachronism; others of his readers, particularly those who are partisans of theological conservativisms of various kinds, tend to believe that he must really hold to the inerrancy of Scripture, or to very high views of the church, or to some other meta-theological position with which such hearty supernaturalism is usually associated.

But Lewis will not be thus associated. He does not espouse fundamentalism or "high-church" views, or a lofty view of the development of Christian doctrine, or a simply experiential anti-intellectualism either. His point is neither to be for any of these nor to be against them. So, too, with scholasticism, neo-scholasticism, and the neo-philosophies of the past few decades. His view is not only a tactical one, namely, of not wishing to give offense to adherents; it is that the large-scale paradigm or model is wrong. That time-honored pattern which suggests that we must think and understand with a second-order scheme is what he is after. That is why the remark already noted (from *The Case for Christianity*) that the theories are not the thing we are asked to accept is so apt. Believing in Christianity is not like that, and the model is wrong. Just as John Locke, the philosopher, had said that we have knowledge only of ideas, leaving it dubious whether we even know things, so the intellectual world, not least the Christian teachers, make us think that we can become Christians only through theological theories. When these prove to be undecidable and ambiguous, then doubting begins to look more honest and religious, and a certain kind of relativism and the invidious business of entertaining a dozen incompatible philosophies and theologies at once looks like the requirement of our enlightened age.

After a while a tolerance of many views develops and such tolerance defines another and new kind of relativism that is supposedly modern and scientific. This survives, however, only if we are sure that the matter of formulating a theory, not least a theological theory, is the one way to know reality. Against the tolerant attitude where every view is accepted "to a certain extent," where every argument is valid "to a certain degree," there a formidable kind of rationality also begins to dissipate. No wonder we get romantics and self-expression advocates, those who proclaim the rights of emotion, who espouse radical subjectivity, the crudities of existentialism, and even that might makes right. It would have been easy for Lewis to move back to an earlier idealism, for there at least, as in some other traditional philosophies, the hope lies in the ability of thought itself to lay hold of genuine transcendentals. Everything else seems to get a standard. It would have been easy, too, for Lewis to latch onto a norm like biblical inerrancy or papal infallibility and then flail the opposition for deviationism. But he did none of these.[11] He choses, instead, the very difficult task of thinking through a long array of literature and of the appropriate situations and circumstances to which these are addressed and in which they are produced.

Lewis's way is the long one. It is the story of his authorship and life. He tries all over again a range of thoughts and circumstances, everything from the vice and virtue teachings of Plato and Aristotle to fairy tales, from the psalms to the apostle Paul, from myths to epic poetry, from allegories to discursive theories, not to become a dilettante or a generalizer but to ascertain by the exploration of the examples and by the testing of himself where both the criteria and the difficulties finally lay. Out of all that something begins to dawn. It is people who become rational, and becoming rational is a life-long process. People can actually discover the rich variety of norms and do so not by being propagandized but by exploring the objective world and discovering how things are.

11. Note his candid remarks in "Scripture," *Reflections on the Psalms,* chap. XI.

By paying attention to the subject one discovers the object. Sown in subjectivity and reaped in objectivity! The human subject is a moral agent and, therefore, it matters enormously what he or she makes of the self. All rational propensities are also a realized function of that human subject. We can never give up the arduous business of tuning up the instrument. We have to decide by hard inquiry what is literal, what is allegorical, fictional, exaggeration, true, symbolic, realistic and, finally, even what is factual. The same can be said about the Bible. There are no easy ways and surely no theories, theological or otherwise, that will enable us to do all this at a stroke.

All the more reason why Lewis's confidence about what he calls the "heavenly realm" is so striking. He says baldly:

> . . . certainly no less than the natural universe and perhaps very much [the heavenly realm] is a realm of objective facts—hard, determinate facts, not to be constructed "a priori," and not to be dissolved into maxims, ideals, values, and the like. One cannot conceive a more completely "given," or if you like, a more "magical," fact than the existence of God as "causa sui."[12]

The point is that the subject has to discover and to learn to be rational. One cannot read that off the clouds or simply apply some rules to one's behavior. There is nothing automatic or facile about becoming aware of norms and being subjected to criteria. This is a delicate and yet an altogether feasible and readily available way to be. Lewis's thrust is chiefly to make us aware of how those simple teachings became compelling and also the facts in the matter. A kind of certainty is available and we need not wallow everlastingly in points of view and the sea of opinions. After a while—if our lives are concentrated and serious—those sayings of a primary variety begin to be facts because they cannot be doubted. When we have worked on our lives in a moral way, assessed and judged them by virtues and

12. C. S. Lewis, *Letters to Malcolm,* p. 104.

commands, we also erase those capacities that keep doubts alive. We become different, not by becoming more credulous and gullible, but by knowing more of who we are and what we want. Within that context, the occasions for querulousness and doubt begin to ebb away; and we see with new eyes and understand where we were once only puzzled, and know where we once only conjectured. This kind of assurance is not given by a theory or by a theology. Lewis's literature is not so much about that in a theoretical mood as it is an occasion for achieving it. This is finally how his fiction supplements his more critical works. And both strands of the authorship are blended in his religious writings.

III

C. S. Lewis's religious literature is different from most written in our century because it is not like the "sawdust" theology of which he complains:

> . . . the way authors can go on discussing how far certain positions are adjustable to contemporary thought, or beneficial in relation to social problems, or "have a future" before them, but never squarely ask what ground we have for supposing them to be true accounts of any objective reality. As if one was trying to make rather than to learn.[13]

All of that suffers not only from the dismal air of being apologetic and obsequious, begging as it were for a hearing, but worse, it purports to give the true account of faith in the wrong mood and medium. Against the assumption of the past few decades, Lewis does not think that second-order discourse, be it theological, anthropological, or otherwise scientific, will give us the true account of religion. The people who look at things and write in this lofty "about" mood, who contrive a language

13. *Ibid.*, p. 104.

about faith have had it their own way in learned circles. The correlative assumption seems to be that poets, believers, lovers, and the virtuous are always expressing a bias, arguing their interest and indulging their idiosyncrasies. The languages of love, of faith, feeling, and a deep moral persuasion are taken to be tainted at their source. Therefore, we think the language in the "of" mood never explains, elucidates, amplifies, or knows the truth. Instead it only "expresses," and lacks the superb intellectual qualities of facticity and truth. It has to be explained, studied, and analyzed, rather than doing any of these itself.

Lewis is eager to deny all of this. He is resolute in the prior claim of poetry itself. To study it requires not the explanation and history of it so much as understanding it enough to be able to put it on as the first-person words of one's own lips. This is the way it is with moral teachings too. Most of all it is the case with the religious and Christian teachings. Such a conviction does not mean that we simply parrot the words in a thoughtless and uncritical way. We do not just memorize verses and everlastingly quote the biblical texts. Rather, it supposes that getting those words on our lips will require that our whole consciousness and manner of looking at the world will also have to change. Thus, new emotions and feelings will be required, and a whole train of new passions and convictions will ensue. Then an appropriate way of thinking about what is the fact will also occur. By such means, we will also find the truth and know objective reality.

Certainly Lewis is right when he says that those people who look "at," as it were from the outside, have simply browbeaten those who look from the inside. His own analogue is helpful. He notes that standing one day in a dark toolshed, he saw a sunbeam filtering through the crack at the top of the door. Looking at it was to see the beam and nothing more; but using that beam of light, he could peer through the crack above the door and see the leaves of a tree and beyond that, the sun itself,

93 million miles away. For Lewis, ideas and words are not something one only looks at; they are the tools for looking at everything else.[14] One looks along the beam and sees the world; one looks at the beam and sees scarcely anything else. The words of poets, of apostles, and of moral sages might sometime have to be examined, but the first requirement and surely the fundamentally rational procedure is to check up on the account that they give when the words and thoughts are used in the same manner as they were with their progenitors. For reasons which are exceedingly obscure, it is now assumed by almost everyone that the account in the "about mood" somehow debunks and refutes the depiction and seeing done from the inside.

This bluntly is the way it is in religious circles too. The task of speaking on behalf of Christian belief in an evangelical and heart-warming way is now made so confoundedly difficult that the intelligentsia conclude that it cannot be done, save by that rare evangelist who is either bigoted and a sham, taking advantage of the multitudes' hunger, or ignorant and hence unaware of all modern knowledge. If what we have said in earlier chapters about Lewis's convictions about literature and people was at all plain, we can now see why he thinks the modern outlook a downright prejudice. It is worse than that—it is something like a philosophical outlook, a general and practiced notion about the logic and shape of all thought. And that is what he is attacking, not by suggesting another and alternative general view, but by proposing that poetry, myths, the Gospels, narrative fiction, and moral teachings really be tried in their own terms again. This is a rediscovery and not an invention. It is a clue to a kind of polymorphic rationality which can be practiced and verified in the reduplication.

Best of all, Lewis both suggests that possibility and then does it. His theology, if that is what one cares to call it, is of a quality with the New Testament literature itself. In fact, it is an imagi-

14. "Meditation in a Toolshed," in *God in the Dock,* pp. 212–16.

native extension of that primary kind of language to all kinds of circumstances that are current and odd to our time. For the same reason, however, that we might have stopped to hear Dr. Samuel Johnson on whatever topic, so we stop to hear Lewis. There is almost always a ring of authority to what is being said, but not the authority of abstract learning or the citation of instances. It is the authority of someone who has found something out about this or that and who tells us not how he feels but the way things are. More than that, his language reflects the fact that we get one kind of experience of a thing when we look at it and an altogether different kind when we think with it. For the language of faith, those plain kerygmatic sayings did vast things for Lewis. They made him appreciate, even relish, his life's work; they reminded him of what he had been seeking all of his life; they proposed a goal and destiny that even the richest imagination could not match.

If a love for a girl can transform an outlook and drastically modify one's behavior, so, too, can the language of the lover change one's seeing, wishing, and hoping. Many things become new; and the deeper the love, the more total the transformation of one's world. One notices things one had never seen before and cherishes the presence of the beloved more than anything else. For Lewis, the force of Christian teachings is so grandiloquent and vast that he learned with it all kinds of strange and new things. Christianity itself began to educate him. His literature is so different, not because it is confessional and about himself, but because he knows what it is like to feel, to think, to judge, to hope, as a Christian. And Christianity is an objective phenomenon—its teachings are already around; Lewis has actually seen it from the inside and therefore has a subjective matter to talk about.

This is why his kind of supernaturalistic faith suddenly seemed so vivid and sharp. We have the distinct impression that he had used all kinds of teachings, looking "with" them not "at" them, and had really discovered God. He knew believing and hoping from the inside. His literature is replete with that firsthand awareness of one who was educated *by* Christianity, not just *to* it. Something like this can be said about his work in poetry and in morals too.

The consequence is that his writing about religious things is also full of appeal to the human heart. Most of us have experienced by early middle age more than enough to give us access to the plays of Shakespeare, Sophocles, and Racine. Usually we have hearts and lives that are full of anxiety, grief, and frustration. If we are articulate at all, we also have a language to articulate our woes and joys as well as to describe them. The appeal of Lewis's religious writing depends in large part upon the ease with which he can address us as we know ourselves in griefs, pleasures, sorrows, and woes, and he makes Christianity congruent with all of that. For that is already the way Christianity and its early literature are. Christians dared to say that their Lord was a Man of Sorrows and acquainted with grief. His appeal is to those crushed by remorse, withered by failure, and shrunken by despair. But there is more. We also are restless for satisfaction, ridden by a lust for life, and zealous for a happiness so perfect that every other joy becomes a foreshadow.

Until the language of faith can begin to construe the manifold of the human heart, it can never quite match up humankind and God. Lewis managed that. He did it not because he had made so many matchless intellectual and theoretical discoveries but because he was courageous enough to acknowledge publicly what most of us surmise in a defeated way so much of our lives. He saw differences and dared their exploitation, even when the weight of the academic surroundings pressed against him.

This was not only, however, a performance on his own behalf. For the striking factor is that he becomes here also a teacher for all the rest of us.

IV

There are two distinctive aspects to Lewis's work as a religious writer that I wish to comment upon here. One is that throughout his works, he writes in such a way as to educate, literally to educe, in his reader most of the capacities and skills that he needs to become faithful, critical, understanding and, in brief, enabled and empowered. We might say that he teaches with suitable indirection and decorum so that we learn not just about poetry, morals, and religion; but, if we have a willing spirit, we can learn there the language "of" poetry, morals, and Christian faith. More than this, we can also acquire the tools and personality qualifications to make use of them. If we have done what was promised in earlier pages, it ought to be clear to the reader that this is not, then, a matter of conditioning nor of subtle manipulation.

It seems rather unusual that our author should be so richly endowed that he could do this at all. Lewis surely did not decide to do anything of the sort, nor do his books ever suggest anything like a lifelong teleology in this direction. Instead, it happened because Lewis wrote his own way to clarity and to conviction. Often his books and articles have a polemical bite to them, mostly when he needs to make his case against the prevailing winds of doctrine. Having traversed his letters at some length and read everything I can find of his published works, it seems to me almost as if gradually he saw that he did not need theories, second-level theologies, and general views, the sort of thing that the sophisticated world of letters and science mostly produces. He did not altogether disparage them, but he found that their role was severely limited. That recognition must have been momentous. It certainly gave his literature a different focus and power.

What he did increasingly see that he needed was both a moral conviction and the little bit of light for the next step. He wanted to be tasteful, to live with relish, to be a master of daily life not its victim, to be upright and just, to be holy and pure. For most of us, these wishes are vagrant, not dominant, and the daily pursuits (and academic ones if we are teachers or scholars) soon push them into second place. This was not the case with Lewis. He put his academic training and skills under the sovereignty of those more fundamental aspirations. He knew what mattered most to himself and to others. That clarity of mind and intention gave him remarkable self-control and confidence. He seldom seemed debilitated by double-mindedness. He never settled for an authorship that only added facts to what we already have.

Therefore, he writes with esthetic, moral, and religious pathos. He has these under control. He knows each domain and never confuses them. He finds Matthew Arnold muddling poetry with religion, I. A. Richards making poetry serve as a surrogate religion, and modern biblical critics reading myths into every sort of Christian writings. Certainly their confusion comes from posing too inclusive a theory, but also from not knowing the languages of poetry and of faith from within. To distinguish them requires that one know each very well. So, too, the modern theologians, who treat the New Testament as if it were only ethics, are illustrating their poverty of sympathetic understanding of the differences between morals and faith, however impressive their argumentation and other kinds of erudition.

This range of Lewis's competencies is what gives him vivaciousness of thought and expression. He is not writing about a form of consciousness he does not share. More than that, he has use for learning in a thousand circumstances and forms. He uses the learning, and the learning never seems to use him. In religious matters this becomes peculiarly appropriate. Lewis was not interested in adding new data to our store of religious knowledge either. He used all the learning and skills he could manage—and they were considerable: a quickness in Greek, a parry in Latin, the felicitous command of literature, the needful critical distinctions—to show us the paramount role of our sensibility itself. We have to be very careful here and stay true to a fundamental contention that also gives symmetry to his literary scholarship.

One of the chief contributions Lewis made as a scholar was to disparage the popular view that the Renaissance and the rise of so-called scientific method reshaped almost completely the mode of Western thought. In his *English Literature in the Sixteenth Century* he shows rather conclusively that those popular views are wrong. In a dozen other contexts, large and small, he does not so much argue a thesis as simply show us by example that when we all become enamored with the contents of our psyche and the cosmology within our subjectivity, we are doomed to triviality and chaos. Soon we indulge nonsense, seek always for "originality," indulge anything in the name of "creativity," and make the self the chief end of life and literature. Unreason is vaunted, and discipline and obedience are thought jejune. Lewis has shown us also that Seneca and Dr. Johnson are far more likely to understand one another than are Robert Burton, an Elizabethan, and Sigmund Freud, a contemporary.

What divides us in sensibility and mode of understanding is not the romantic movement alone; it is the proclivity of that movement, plus other factors, to turn us from a God-centered and orderly universe to a self, impulsive and ruleless, and never quite ordered. "But somewhere between us and *Persuasion,* the chasm runs."[15] Today we are not easily persuaded to look for God and for moral absolutes. A kind of cultural agreement, call it the effects of romanticism, has made most of us think Christianity, along with poetry, is only a tinkering with the inner life. Lewis's scholarship and criticism brings that view to severe examination. We all happen into this popular mode of con-

15. C. S. Lewis, "De Descriptione Temporum," in *Selected Literary Essays,* p. 7.

sciousness if we are not exceedingly careful.

A deeper thrust in the Lewis literature, however, is the amplification and exemplification of the first page of his *Allegory of Love.* He says there:

> Humanity does not pass through phases as a train passes through a station: being alive, it has the privilege of always moving yet never leaving anything behind. Whatever we have been, in some sort we are still.

Despite that effect of construing everything psychologically and thereby effecting a breach with earlier centuries, a modern person is not as far from Christian things as the temper of the age would suggest. Lewis's Christian writings do the apologetic task in another manner altogether. Indeed he is concerned with eternal verities and an absolute God, but Lewis does not believe that showing that we have eternal truths and proofs of God's existence will suffice. Those eternal truths and indubitable proofs have a way of being dreadfully uninteresting and almost without point. That God-centered universe and the celestial harmonies make no appeal.

Right here is Lewis's difference made explicit. He shows us that what we have been, we still are. A striking feature of his authorship is to show that Christianity has not been left that far behind. It is the mode of consciousness and the sensibility that have been modified, but not because of new discoveries or indelibly conceived truths. The changes in sensibility are part of the story of the freedom of man. Those changes are not necessitated and are not a function of general laws. They can be effected from within. Therefore, Lewis's religion literature becomes a long kind of *praeparatio evangelica* rather than evangelism itself. [16] This was necessary in order to create an audience. The audience was not, finally, his group of fans, nor those who were titillated by his novelties. They were those who discovered anew

16. *Letters,* p. 193.

their potentialities and wishes, who identified themselves in more historically familiar ways, and who swept the popular self-descriptions aside and discovered what was already there.

That preparation for the evangel is a modest task and it goes on in Lewis's pages in a variety of ways. Lewis is like Dr. Johnson, who thought it was always a fresh and enlivening discovery to learn that "prudence and justice are virtues, and excellences, of all times and places." Like him, too, Lewis shows us that knowledge and theories "are not the great or the frequent business of the human mind. . . . we are perpetually moralists, but we are geometricians only by chance."[17] With Lewis, we ought not to lose our taste for epic poetry, but to educate it; we can also rediscover the fairy tale and not have it vanquished by getting old; we might even relish again the youthful ardor we had for hopes for ourselves and all mankind. Lewis thinks that a recovery of all of these, but especially of moral sensitivity, also spells the recovery of the capacity to believe in God.

This enlivening and straightening of human sensibility is part of another and longer story. We can all become part of a crooked and perverse generation by merely going along and being conformists to the modern scene. A profound and truly deep and many-sided transformation takes place in Lewis's picture of what it is for people to be knowers and, even more, a knower and friend of God. Despite Lewis's disclaimers to the contrary, there is a new epistemology emerging in his literature. The surprising aspect of all this is that he does not do it by argument or by a direct confrontation with what might look like rival epistemologies. Nowhere is there what one might call a theory of reality or a metaphysics. This is not to say that God is not real or that God cannot, in a certain modified sense, be known.

17. Samuel Johnson, "The Life of Milton" in *Lives of the Poets,* I (London: Oxford University Press, reprinted 1973), p. 72.

Lewis's reflections are so guarded and so carefully wrought that a morphology of the thinker is both shown in his works and elicited by them. That morphology makes most of the popular scientism, the ordinary kinds of positivism, the reliance upon second-level theologies look like exaggerations and unnecessary intellectual excrescences. We discover, instead, that we can know, believe, and be certain, where previously there was only a wild panoply of views. The logics of thinking develop also from within. They are confirmed, however, also from without. They fit the world, people, and the gospel. A kind of orthodoxy and ordering of reflection is our reward, not solely our goad. This is also the way it is with Christian things. "Mere Christianity" turns out to be not a burden at all, but that kind of ordering and enlivening of our lives that means that daily existence becomes a joy and being canonical the promise of eternal felicity.

I would be remiss if I failed to mark that Lewis had also discovered for himself the remarkable pleasure we could all share in being thinking human beings. Dr. Johnson once said that a person who was tired of London would also be tired of human life itself. Lewis did not share the *angst* that is so celebrated by the arts and the religion of our day. He did know about despair, but he knew it was transitory and not at all a cosmic necessity. The grand epistemology of his pages imbues the reader with the confidence that in thinking right, we also live right. We can also say that in living right, we will also think right. This novel notion, so old that it is embarrassing to think about its history, is still surprising to all of us. We are so used to thinking in other categories that we think we can have the truth without being happy and that we can be happy without knowing the truth.

Lewis's pages have the depth here of the suggestive remarks of Simone Weil and maybe, too, of Ludwig Wittgenstein. Once more we are reminded, both by the gospel itself (that Lewis only transmits) and by Lewis's reflections of a formal sort (on metaphor, allegory, "words," stories, poems, criticisms, and more) that form and content, thought and behavior, subjective and objective cannot be long separated. The gospel itself is a call to a new integrity and a new life, and also a new thought-life.

The things in Lewis's account of human life that are also the best are clearly the most costly. The gospel cost God the life of Jesus Christ. We do not have to sacrifice our intellects in order to be redeemed, but we do have to be converted, even in thought. Lewis gives us a clue to the transformation that is like a restoration. Once effected, it is as if the unbidden reward is a world that once more makes sense. Our daily life hides a longing so pervasive, a need so powerful, that nothing save God, immortality, and redemption will assuage them.

In brief, there is a felicitous synthesis of factors in the personality itself. Our emotions can be schooled and trained along with our thoughts. The picture of the life of Christian discipleship that is drawn by Lewis is one that cannot, at the long last, fail to attract. It supposes that our thoughts need no longer enslave us in a hypothetical mood, nor our emotions keep us everlastingly in a state of anxiety. By choosing the small issues first, the large questions also find their resolution. This happy coincidence is plotted by Lewis's considerations of how we come to think, feel, and know; but it is also promised and effected in our lives by God's uncovenanted mercy and grace. No wonder, then, that C. S. Lewis could serve us all so well.